Faces of Love
Hafez and the Poets of Shiraz

Introduced and Translated by
Dick Davis

MAGE PUBLISHERS

Some of these translations have previously appeared in *Able Muse, Parnassus, Poetry,* and the *Raintown Review.* The author is grateful to the National Endowment for the Arts for the award of a grant to translate the poems of Jahan Malek Khatun.

Library of Congress Cataloging-in-Publication Data

Faces of love : Hafez and the poets of Shiraz / introduced and translated by Dick Davis. -- 1st hardcover ed.   p. cm.

Includes bibliographical references and indexes.

ISBN 1-933823-48-8 (hardcover : alk. paper)

1. Persian poetry—747-1500—Translations into English. 2. Hafiz, 14th cent.—Translations into English. 3. Jahan Malik Khatun, 14th cent.—Translations into English. 4. ʿUbayd Zakani, Nizam al-Din, d. ca. 1370—Translations into English. I. Davis, Dick. II. Hafiz, 14th cent. Divan. English. Selections. III. Jahan Malik Khatun, 14th cent. Divan. English. Selections. IV. ʿUbayd Zakani, Nizam al-Din, d. ca. 1370 Poems. English. Selections.
PK6449.E5F33 2012
891'.5511--dc23

                                        2012016581

First Hardcover Print on Demand Edition
ISBN 13: 978-1-949445-01-5

Mage books are available at bookstores, through the Internet or directly from the publisher
as@mage.com
visit Mage online at www.mage.com

Cooking in Iran: Regional Recipes and Kitchen Secrets
Najmieh Batmanglij

Joon: Persian Cooking Made Simple
Najmieh Batmanglij

Food of Life: Ancient Persian and Modern Iranian Cooking and Ceremonies
Najmieh Batmanglij

Silk Road Cooking: A Vegetarian Journey
Najmieh Batmanglij

From Persia to Napa: Wine at the Persian Table
Najmieh Batmanglij, Dick Davis, Burke Owens

Savushun: A Novel about Modern Iran
Simin Daneshvar / Translated by M.R. Ghanoonparvar

A Social History of Sexual Relations in Iran
Willem Floor

Bushehr: City, Society, and Trade, 1797–1947
Willem Floor

A Social History of Sexual Relations in Iran
Willem Floor

Engelbert Kaempfer: Exotic Attractions in Persia, 1684–1688: Travels & Observations
Translated from the Latin by Willem Floor and Colette Ouahes

The Persian Garden: Echoes of Paradise
Mehdi Khansari / M. R. Moghtader / Minouch Yavari

The Persian Sphinx: Amir Abbas Hoveyda and the Iranian Revolution
Abbas Milani

For Afkham, Najmieh and Mohammad,
Mariam and Mehri, Zal and Rostam

THE PRONUNCIATION OF PERSIAN NAMES

Persian names are pronounced with a more even stress than is common in English, which sounds to an English speaker's ear as though the last syllable is being slightly stressed. There are two "a" sounds in Persian: a long "a" like the "a" in the British pronunciation of "father"; and a short "a" like the "a" in "cat." In Hafez the "a" is long; in Jahan the first "a" is short, and the second "a" long; in Malek the "a" is short; in Khatun the "a" is long. The "Kh" of Khatun is pronounced like the Scottish "ch" in "loch." The "a" in Abu is short; that in Es'haq and Bos'haq is long; in Mozaffar each "a" is short; in Mobarez the "a" is long. Obayd is pronounced more or less as though it were the English word "obeyed." Each "a" in Zakani is long. The "q" at the end of "Es'haq" and "Bos'haq" is pronounced like a guttural "g," far back in the throat. The apostrophe in Es'haq and Bos'haq indicates only that the "s" and "h" sounds are pronounced separately, as in "mishandle," not together as in "ashen."

Contents

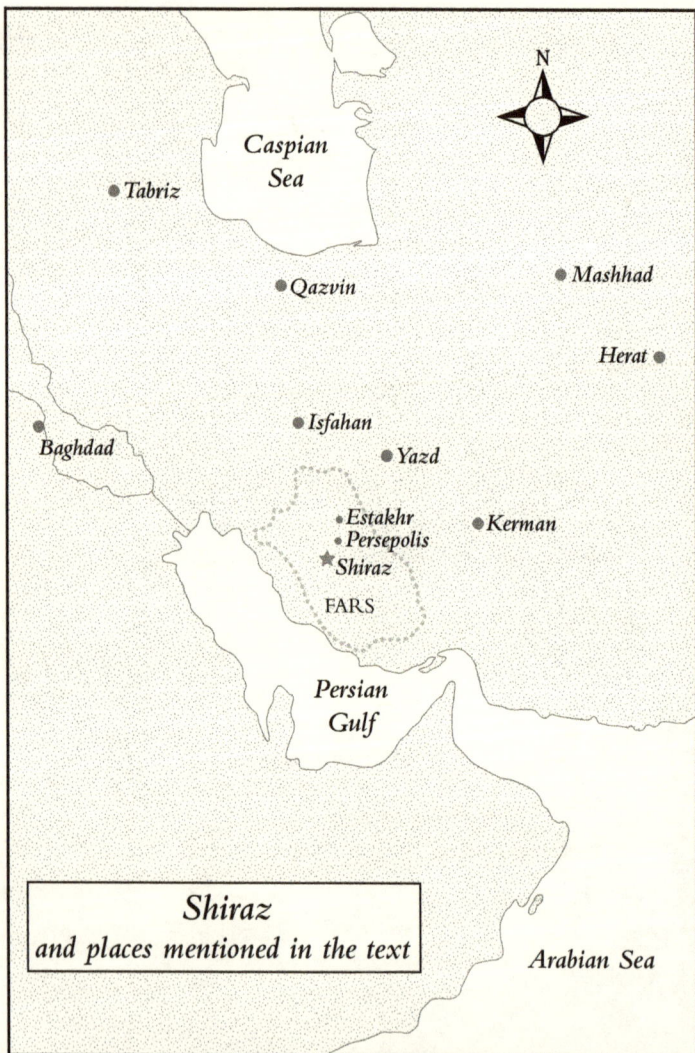

Caspian
Sea

N

• Tabriz

• Qazvin

• Mashhad

Herat •

• Isfahan

Baghdad •

• Yazd

• Estakhr
• Persepolis
★ Shiraz

• Kerman

FARS

Persian
Gulf

Shiraz
and places mentioned in the text

Arabian Sea

Introduction

Shiraz is the capital of Fars, the southern central province of Persia/Iran that was the home of two of its greatest pre-Islamic imperial dynasties, the Achaemenids, who established the Persian Empire and are known in western history as the Asian antagonists of ancient Greece, and the Sasanians, who fought against Rome and Byzantium until their empire was destroyed during the Arab/Islamic conquest of the country in the seventh century. During this pre-Islamic period, Shiraz was a place of very minor importance, overshadowed at first by the nearby Achaemenid palace of Persepolis, and later, when this fell into ruin, by the imperial city of Estakhr. Shiraz, at this time though, does have one claim to fame; it is one of the archaeological sites that show the earliest traces of systematic wine-making in the Near East. It was not until the Islamic period that Shiraz became the capital of the province; this seems to have been a deliberate strategy on the part of the Islamic conquerors, as the more established towns of southern Iran, like Estakhr and Isfahan, were for a long time fiercely resistant to their new rulers, and also for a while to the new religion that they brought with them.

The green, fertile plain on which Shiraz is located is admirably suited for agriculture, including wine production, and this is in stark contrast to the aridity of much of the Persian landscape. The city nestles at the foot of the Zagros Mountains, and its elevation of over 5,000 feet above sea-level has ensured it a comparatively mild and equable climate compared with much of the rest of Iran. The pass through the mountains to the north affords a sudden sight of the city lying below in its green splendor; in the Middle Ages, this view was thought to be so strikingly beautiful that the pass became known by the name "Allahu Akbar" ("God is Great"), from the phrase travellers were said to shout out when they saw Shiraz and its orchards and gardens spread out below them.

Shiraz prospered in the medieval period; it became a trading center with direct links to the Persian Gulf to the south, and so to imported goods from India and the Arabian peninsula, and its merchant class, centered on the city's bazaar, became wealthy and important in the government of Fars. Its commercial life was not unlike that of the great mercantile cities of medieval Italy, such as Venice and Genoa, although on a more modest scale, because Shiraz for a long time remained a comparatively small city. As in its Italian counterparts, at the highest levels of society the city's wealth resulted in a great deal of artistic patronage, and the efflorescence of a culture of self-conscious luxury and elegance. One result of this artistic patronage was the development of a distinctively Shirazi school of poetry; in the thirteenth century the Shirazi poet Sa'di (c.1213–92) was considered the greatest living Persian poet, and from this time on Shiraz's reputation as a city of poetry was assured.

Sa'di was followed by various other poets associated with the city, including Khaju Kermani (1280–1352), who, despite his name, which identifies him as coming from the city of Kerman, made his home in Shiraz, and whose poetry provides a kind of link between that of Sa'di and that of Hafez and his contemporaries. Khaju's poetry has had the unfortunate fate of being overshadowed by the work of both his illustrious predecessor, and his even more illustrious successor. Some of the great families of the city were also known for their interest in Sufism, the heterodox mysticism of Islam, and the Sufism and the poetry often tended to become mixed up with one another, which is not surprising as it was the wealthy who provided poets with patronage. This literary Sufism has varying degrees of seriousness in the work of different poets: sometimes it seems sincere, and central to what the poet is saying; sometimes it can seem little more than the deployment of a fashionable rhetoric.

The three Shirazi poets whose work is featured in this book, Hafez, Jahan Malek Khatun, and Obayd-e Zakani, lived at the same time (the mid fourteenth century), and certainly knew of one another – Obayd wrote at least two poems about Jahan Khatun, and Jahan Khatun quotes Hafez in one of her poems. It's extremely likely that, during the 1340s and early 1350s at least, they also knew one another personally. The poetic life of the city during this period centered on the court of the ruling family, the Injus; Jahan Khatun was an Inju princess, while her uncle, Abu Es'haq, the head of the family and the ruler of the city, was a great patron of poets. Both Hafez and Obayd were among the recipients of his patronage (they each wrote praise poems dedicated to him), and both are likely to have been frequent visitors at his court. Perhaps because her parents had no sons, Jahan Khatun had received what was then an unusual education for a woman, even an aristocratic one – she had been taught to read and write, and was a highly accomplished poet whose verses brought her a local fame. The women of the largely Mongol families that ruled Iran during the thirteenth and fourteenth centuries, and which included the Inju dynasty, were much less secluded than was usual in other Moslem courts of the period, and they often took an active part in their courts' social life; it seems reasonable to assume that a princess who had access to her uncle's court, and who wrote poetry, would make sure that she was there whenever Hafez – the most famous poet of the town, not to say the whole of Iran – was present. Whether she enjoyed the company of Obayd-e Zakani is more doubtful. His verses about her are not at all complimentary, and he was famous for the satirical, scabrous, and often obscene nature of his poetry; even the relatively easygoing Injus might have thought his company was a bit much for a well-brought-up young woman. Still, it is likely that Jahan Khatun and Obayd had an at least nodding acquaintance, as Obayd too was, for a while, a member of the poetic gatherings convened by Jahan Khatun's uncle, Abu Es'haq.

An indulgent ruler, a poet-princess who was his niece, the most famous poet of the age, and a somewhat disreputable hanger-on who also wrote verses, all meeting together for poetic gatherings in a city famous for its gardens, nightingales and roses, its generally mild and gentle climate, and the pleasures of its open-air social gatherings – all this sounds rapturously idyllic in its elegance and charm, and no doubt, for some of the time, it was. But the fourteenth century was an extremely violent and dangerous period in Iran's history, and although Shiraz could claim in some ways to be something of a haven (it had largely escaped the depredations of the thirteenth-century Mongol invasion of the country, for example, as it was also to escape the worst consequences of the conquests by Timur the Lame – Tamburlaine – in the 1380s, in both cases by astutely accommodating political moves on the part of its rulers), it still saw an immense amount of bloodshed and political chaos of a kind that directly affected our three poets, and came close to killing at least one of them. In one five-year period, for example (1339-44), the government of Shiraz and the province of Fars changed hands no less than eight times; each time blood ran in the palaces and usually in the streets too. If Shiraz was fortunate enough to escape the most spectacularly destructive wars that engulfed much of Iran in the thirteenth and fourteenth centuries, the fierce in-fighting of local would-be ruling families was more than enough to ensure constant periods of nightmarish political instability.

The careers of two families, the Injus and the Mozaffarids, are of particular importance in helping us understand the historical reality that lies behind the poems of Hafez, Jahan Khatun, and Obayd-e Zakani. The Inju prince Masud Shah succeeded his father – the dynasty's founder – as king of the area in 1336. He was driven out by ambitious rivals in 1339, and various claimants to the throne squabbled over the rulership of Shiraz and Fars until 1342, when Masud Shah returned at the head of a sizable army and regained control of the province. His triumph was short-lived though, as he was murdered by a subordinate within a year. His younger brother, Abu Es'haq, avenged his death in 1343, ruling Shiraz and its environs until 1353, when he was in turn driven out of Shiraz by the Mozaffarid warlord, Mobarez al-din. The deposed Inju king fled to Isfahan, but was captured there by forces allied with Mobarez al-din, who had his royal prisoner brought back to Shiraz and put to death in its main square.

As the new king of Shiraz, Mobarez al-din could not have been more different from Abu Es'haq, either in temperament or as a ruler. He was, at least outwardly, fanatically religious, and also extremely brutal. The historian Khandamir (1475–1534) recounts an anecdote that yokes together his piety and ruthlessness. A couple of prisoners were brought into Mobarez al-din's presence while he was praying; the ruler completed the section of prayer on which he was engaged, stood up, cut off the prisoners' heads, and returned to his prayers. The same historian reports how Mobarez al-din boasted to his son that he had personally killed over 800 people. The most obvious effect of Mobarez al-din's rule, apart from the terror it inspired, was his strict enforcement of Islamic religious prohibitions. Wine-shops, which had flourished during Abu Es'haq's lax not to say dissipated reign, were closed, both wine and music were forbidden, and severe sobriety became the order of the day. Mobarez al-din also doesn't seem to have been very interested in poetry: at one point he considered having the grave of Sa'di destroyed, because he thought the great poet's verses weren't Islamic enough. The Shirazis, who had (and to some extent still have, despite the Islamic Revolution of 1979) a reputation for not holding back when it comes to enjoying life's pleasures, referred to their new ruler by the contemptuous nickname "the Morals Officer."

After five years of Mobarez al-din's rule in Shiraz, his dour brutality proved too much even for his son, Shah Shoja, who had his father blinded, deposed, and imprisoned. Shah Shoja finally sent the old man off to a prison in Bam (near Kerman, Mobarez al-din's base before he captured Shiraz), where he died. To the relief of at least some sections of the population, Shah Shoja reversed his father's draconian anti-pleasure policies, and wine and music once again emerged from the shadows where they had been hidden away. Jahan Khatun made her peace with the son (she has some poems that praise him), as did Hafez and Obayd-e Zakani – who had apparently also considered discretion to be the better part of valor and hightailed it out of Shiraz shortly after Mobarez al-din took over – and all three of them returned to the city. Shah Shoja ruled Shiraz for well over twenty years (from 1358 to 1384, with a brief inter-regnum during 1364–6); by the end of his reign, Obayd-e Zakani was dead, and both Jahan Khatun and Hafez were nearing the end of their lives.

These political events are clearly reflected in Jahan Khatun's poems, as might be expected, given that she and her family were so deeply involved in Shiraz's dynastic upheavals, but they are also present as a kind of ground bass in the poetry of both Hafez and Obayd-e Zakani. Most obviously, both poets praise Abu Es'haq, and both express disdain and loathing for Mobarez al-din and the consequences of his reign on the life of their city. More subtly, a constantly repeated refrain in the work of each of them (very different though their poems can be in other ways) is that the world is not to be trusted, and that living in relative seclusion, far from court, is the wisest and the safest course. Although it is a commonplace of medieval Persian verse, this apprehension of the often terrifying instability of human affairs was surely reinforced by the political chaos all three poets witnessed and must to some extent have experienced.

THE CONVENTIONS OF FOURTEENTH-CENTURY PERSIAN LYRIC POETRY

A much more pervasive influence than political events on the content and atmosphere of these writers' verses was the set of conventions associated with the type of poetry they were writing. Such conventions always exert a strong pull, whether conscious or unconscious, on what a writer feels can be said in a poem, as well as on the ways in which it seems appropriate to say these things. When we read poems from a culture whose genre conventions resemble those of our own, the constraints that genre suggests are perhaps not especially obvious, because we have already internalized them as "natural" (as when an English speaker reads Italian sonnets, for example; there are differences, but they fall within a recognizable range of what can be expected in a sonnet). But the case is quite different when we read poems from a culture with unfamiliar genre conventions; here the "recognizable range" is lacking, and we can feel lost. The conventions of fourteenth-century Persian lyric verse – and most of the poems included in this book can be characterized as lyrics of one kind or another – are not especially close to European lyric conventions (although there is perhaps more overlap than might at first sight be apparent). We need to make some attempt to familiarize ourselves with this unfamiliarity if we are to be able to see what it is that these poets are saying, and why they are saying such things in the particular ways that they do.

Perhaps the most fundamental fact about Persian lyric verse of this period is that it is court poetry, which means that its rhetoric is the rhetoric of praise poetry. Poetry exalting the sovereign and his powerful ministers and friends was in great demand, and produced the highest rewards for those who could excel at it. The most obvious lyric form, the ghazal, began as an offshoot of the praise poem, as a kind of lyrical introduction to it, which then became detached as an independent form, in much the same way that in the west the overture began as an introduction to an opera, but then became an independent piece which could stand alone. The rhetoric of the ghazal was still, in effect, the rhetoric of the praise poem. This had two results: 1) a ghazal's rhetoric slips easily into hyperbole (princes can always believe the best of themselves, and lovers too apparently); and 2) a ghazal is virtually always concerned with a relationship between a speaker and an addressee in which the addressee is conceived of as infinitely superior to the speaker (the relationship is virtually never one of equivalence, or of the speaker feeling superior to the addressee, except as a reversal of expectation or as a joke). That is, the relationship is basically that of a courtier to his prince, and the rhetoric in which it is expressed ultimately derives from rhetoric considered to be appropriate to such a relationship. The addressee of a ghazal can be a beloved/lover, a patron, or God. In the work of some poets, it's crystal clear which of these three is being evoked; in the work of others, the situation is more ambiguous and a whole poem can be read as addressed to either a lover or to God, or perhaps to a patron. In still other poems, the verse can seem to glide from one referent to another – at times it seems that a lover is addressed, at times God, at times a patron. This indeterminacy can seem irritating to a reader, who may be impatiently asking himself, "Well, which is it?" But such implied ambiguity of reference was a prized strategy for medieval Persian poets, something regarded as particularly the province of poetry.

This seems fairly distant from the conventions of European verse, but in reality it isn't that far away from some medieval and Renaissance European practices. To go back to the analogy of the sonnet, Giles Fletcher in the introduction to his sonnet sequence *Licia,* published in 1593, wrote:

> If thou muse what my Licia is: take her to be some Diana, at the least chaste; or some Minerva; no Venus – fairer far. It may be she is learning's image, or some heavenly wonder, which the precisest may not mislike. Perhaps under that name I have shadowed Discipline. It may be I mean that kind courtesy which I found at the patroness of these poems; it may be some college. It may be my conceit, and portend nothing.

In effect, Fletcher is saying his "Licia" might be a mistress or a divinity ("some heavenly wonder"), or an emblem of learning or poetic genius ("Discipline"), or an acknowledgment of patronage, or an institution, or simply "my conceit, and portending nothing." Among his alternatives Fletcher includes a lover, a divine being, and a patron, and he refuses to be pinned down between them. These three – lover, God, patron – were the alternatives a Persian poet also played with in lyric verse, and the possibility is always there in a Persian lyric as well as in Fletcher's sonnets that the subject is simply "my conceit . . . nothing," that is, no more than an exercise in rhetorical skill.

Perhaps because the speaker's mind is conceived of as being wholly focused on the poem's subject, to the exclusion of everything else, this subject can be referred to as both "you" and "he" in the course of a poem. This can be confusing for the western reader, who usually expects a "you" and a "he" in the one poem to refer to two different people. Sometimes in a Persian poem they do, but very often they don't. To further complicate things, sometimes more than one person is referred to as "you" (the reader might be so addressed, for example, as well as the poem's addressee); sometimes more than one person is referred to as "he" (the beloved, but also a rival). A reader of Persian lyric poetry has to be alert to the possibilities; as a rule of thumb, if both the "he" and the "you" are extravagantly praised, the odds are they are referring to the same person, the subject of the poem. Although the device seems to be relatively rare in European poetry after the medieval period, this use of both "you" and "he" to refer to the same person was present in both western Classical poetry (the Greek critic Longinus remarks on it) and in biblical verse (in Psalm 23, for example, God is referred to at first as "He" and then, as the psalm proceeds, as "You").

This shifting from second person to third person and perhaps back again, together with the sometimes apparently ambiguous identity of the addressee from moment to moment in the poem, are both similar to a third kind of strategy that, to a western reader, can seem equally disjunctive. Run-on lines are extremely rare in medieval Persian lyric poetry, and each line constitutes, normally, a complete thought unto itself; the apparent disjunctions can come when one moves from line to line – how one line is connected with its predecessor or successor is sometimes not immediately obvious. A sudden shift in what is apparently being talked about is a prized strategy in such poems, and it is the reader's job to ferret out the underlying continuity. One way to approach such poems is to think of them as meditations on a theme, with each line (sometimes groups of lines) approaching the theme from a slightly different angle. The theme might be mutability, for example, and the poem could open with a few lines on the fickleness of the beloved; then there might be a line on the fall of princes, and an apparent excursion for a line or two on ancient pre-Islamic kings; then the poem could return to the fickle lover, and perhaps close with a hope that the poet, who is referred to by name, will be delivered from mutability in some way. It is usual, though not obligatory, for such poems to close with a mention of the poet's name; this can be spoken in the first person, or addressed in the second, or referred to in the third person as if it represented someone quite different from the poem's speaker.

So far I have been referring, deliberately, to "he" rather than "she" when talking about the addressee in these poems. Persian pronouns have no gender distinctions, so that the same word may be translated as "he," "she," or "it." In addition, Persian poetry, when it focuses on physical appearance, only occasionally mentions sexual characteristics (such as a girl's breasts, or a boy's incipient beard). Descriptions of beauty tend to be androgynous, ambisexual; there is usually no way of telling whether a boy or a girl is being talked about. But scholars have generally assumed that, in reality, we are fairly safe in assuming that a medieval Persian ghazal's subject, if it is a beloved, is a boy. The Iranian scholar Sirus Shamisa goes so far as to write that, "the beloved in . . . the independent (Persian) love poem is a boy ninety percent of the time."[1] There is a curious gender distinction in medieval Persian poetic genres: narrative poems such as romances, of which there are many, are virtually always about heterosexual relationships; short lyrical poems tend to be about pederastic ones. The speaker of a short lyric is, all other things being equal, assumed to be a male adult, and the addressee is assumed to be a male adolescent or boy. This has European precedents and parallels, of course: a great deal of Latin and especially Greek lyric poetry was addressed to boys, and Latin poetry

1. Sirus Shamisa, *Sayr-e ghazal dar sh`er-e farsi az aghaz ta emruz* (Tehran: Entesharat-e Ferdowsi, 1362/1983), p. 34.

to boys continued to be written into the Middle Ages.[2] The practice seems more or less to cease in Europe around the time that poetry began to be written in the European vernacular languages, and the two developments may be connected (it was fine for the educated to hear about such things, but God forbid they should reach the ears of the laity). However, there were still, occasionally, poems written to boys well into the Renaissance (by which time it was of course dangerous to commit such notions to print – sodomy was a capital offence in much of Europe): Richard Barnfield's *Certain Sonnets* (1595) and his poem *The Affectionate Shepherd* (1594) are both, albeit rather coyly, about – among other things – the love of boys; Marlowe in one or two passages from his plays and poems makes it quite clear that he finds boys sexy. For such preoccupations Persian poetry had a prestigious precedent much closer to home, in Arabic poetry; among many others, the eight-century poet Abu Nawas, whose mother was Persian and who grew up in a linguistically and culturally hybrid Arab-Persian milieu, was notorious for his poems to boys.

---

2. A number of critics, including Ernst Curtius in *European Literature and the Latin Middle Ages,* translated by Willard Trask (Princeton: Princeton University Press, 1973) have drawn attention to a considerable continuity of rhetoric and themes between late antique/Hellenistic literature and medieval Islamic literature, and the lyric treatment of pederasty is one instance of many. Whether this is simply a case of Hellenistic literary traditions persisting in the Near East, or the result of the fact that much of Hellenistic rhetoric was itself in origin "Asiatic" (as was acknowledged by the literature itself), or, as seems most likely, some combination of the two, is unclear.

However, a consideration of the Classical precedent perhaps suggests that the issue is not simply a question of "These poems are about boys and that's that." We tend to pigeonhole sexuality, taking it for granted that most people are heterosexual, some people homosexual, and an indeterminate number bisexual. This was clearly not how the issue was seen in the ancient world. Horace, for example, refers to both boys and girls in his poems apparently impartially; what's more to the point is that he seems to take this for granted, as if he assumes this would be everyone's practice and preference (or lack of preference). In his satires he says he has "a thousand passions for girls, a thousand passions for boys" and in his odes he names specific boys and girls for whom he feels such passions. Taken together, his erotic poems imply that he was quite happy to have lovers of either sex, as long as they were young and pretty. Martial also has poems to both boys and girls, and even Ovid, who has been considered as a kind of prototype of a later emphatic European heterosexuality (no male poet had taken women's emotional and erotic lives so seriously before, or had seemed so interested in them), wrote in his *Amores* that his concerns could center on "Either a boy, or a pretty girl with long hair."

Interestingly enough, the one Persian poet who repeatedly breaks the taboo on mentioning the sexuality of partners other than in an unspecific androgynous way, is Obayd-e Zakani. Seemingly delighted to talk about sexual characteristics obsessively and at length, he, like Horace, indicates that he was quite happy to have lovers of either sex, again preferably if they were young and pretty. It's also significant in this context that when the princess Jahan

Khatun writes love poems in which a lover is identified by gender, she seems to be talking about a heterosexual relationship. (As we'll see, this is given a bizarre twist by the fact that she often writes as "the man" and the addressee is the woman; nevertheless, the point remains that Jahan Khatun clearly sees the ghazal as a vehicle for celebrating heterosexual as well as homoerotic relationships.) Despite the fact that the conventions of the short love poem in Persian presuppose a pederastic relationship (and it's true that, when on the rare occasions gender identity or sexual characteristics are mentioned in such poems, it's usually clear that a boy rather than a girl is being referred to), I believe it is a mistake to be too dogmatic about this. In the same way that some Victorian commentators and translators tended to bowdlerize these poems by making them always about girls, a blanket insistence that they are always about boys seems to me to be equally tendentious. I believe the situation was probably similar to that which we find in Horace and Obayd (and to some extent Jahan Khatun): both genders are being talked about, sometimes one, sometimes the other, and sometimes it isn't of major importance which – the real subject is longing and desire, polymorphous and overwhelming – and the lack of gender specificity in Persian makes this not only possible but likely.

The most obvious Arab precedent for the conventions of the pederastic lyric in Persian, Abu Nawas (756–814), provides a precedent for another motif that is extremely common in medieval Persian lyric poems, the celebration of wine drinking, often to the point of drunkenness. Again, the fact that these are court poems is significant. Iran had been a Moslem country, nominally since the seventh century, and actually (in the sense that the vast majority of the country's inhabitants had converted by this time) since at least the tenth century, and wine drinking is of course forbidden by Islam. But the prohibition never really took in the Persian courts. As is clear from many pre-Islamic stories that survived the conquest, the courts were centers of wine drinking, often to excess. Local Persian dynasties in the early Islamic period tended to derive their legitimacy from a claimed descent from pre-Islamic kings or heroes, and at their courts the kings assiduously carried on many ancient traditions, in so far as they were aware of them, and these sometimes included wine drinking. They were saying, in effect, "This is a part of our culture; get over it." From the eleventh to the fourteenth centuries, Iran was overrun by successive waves of invaders from Central Asia; many of these came from hard-drinking cultures, and so the courts of the conquerors remained places where wine was flagrantly and often excessively drunk. It may be that the large mass of the populace acquiesced in the Islamic ban on wine, but in general the courts didn't, and the populace of the towns in which the courts were located, taking their cue from the local aristocracy, often didn't either. Though there were always exceptions, such as kings who became seriously religious for one reason or another, one gets the impression that for a monarch to ban wine from his court was thought to be a bit of a social faux pas; something a jumped-up brutal parvenu like Mobarez al-din might do.

Wine and boys are associated together in the figure of the wine-server *(saqi)* or adolescent who serves the wine, who, it is implied, is often also an object of desire to the speaker of a poem (it's possible that – exceptionally – the wine-server might sometimes have been a young woman). Again there is a precedent in Abu Nawas's poems, which celebrate the pleasures of both wine and beautiful boys, and associate the two together. And again, ancient and Hellenistic Greek culture provides a parallel and a precedent, going back at least as far as the fourth century BCE, to Plato's *Symposium*. The frisson of transgression generated by Islam's ban both on wine and on boys as lovers could be part of the attraction.[3] As the eleventh-century poet Manuchehri puts it:

> I like my slave-boy and my wine glass
> > This is no place for blame or contempt
> I know that both are forbidden
> > It's this very "forbidden" that makes
> > them so pleasurable.

There is no getting away from the fact that both wine and the love of boys were and are taboo in orthodox Islam, and equally there is no getting away from the fact that medieval Persian poems contain a great many references to both of them. One way of dealing with this was (and is) to say that the poems are not really about wine and boys at all, but about something much more respectable, such as the love of God. Once again, the precedent of Plato comes to mind, *Phaedrus* in particular ("The love of boys is actually a step towards the divine ... ").

---

3. Willem Floor, *A Social History of Sexual Relations in Iran* (Washington, D.C.: Mage Publishers, 2008).

This strategy can seem both evasive and casuistic, but in our desire to call a spade a spade we have to tread with caution. The tradition of explaining the secular as an allegory of the spiritual is an ancient one in the Middle East, and it cannot be dismissed out of hand as being inapplicable in this case. The biblical *Song of Songs*, which at first glance seems to most contemporary readers to be about secular love and desire, was for over a thousand years considered to be, by Jewish and Christian commentators alike, an allegory of divine love (for Israel, for the church, for the human soul). It was only in the sixteenth century that a French writer, Sébastien Castellion, won some support for what to us is the "obvious" literal, secular interpretation. Such an interpretation had not appeared to be "obvious" to anyone before; merely, perhaps, reductively beside the point.

The interpretation of Persian poetry that apparently deals with secular love and wine as being in reality mystical and Sufi in its subject matter was well established by the fourteenth century. In the previous century the Sufi poet Eraqi had written a glossary of the secular terms he had used in his own poetry, explaining what was "actually" – that is, mystically/in Sufi terms – meant by them. A number of other glossaries and commentaries, with the same intention of explaining apparently secular poetry in terms of a Sufi/mystical content, were subsequently written by other poets and mystics, the most famous of which was the poet Shabestari's *Golshan-e Raz* ("The Rose Garden of Secrets"), written in 1311, a few years before Hafez was born. If our poets were indeed interested in Sufism, they were heirs to this tradition, and could draw on it at will.

And yet it is undeniable that a great deal of perfectly real wine was drunk in the courts and cities where some of this supposedly Sufi poetry was written, and it's also undeniable that Sufis periodically got themselves into trouble over their excessive attachment to all too tangibly flesh-and-blood adolescents (including, it seems, Eraqi himself, for all his claims that the boys in his poems were allegorical). The assumption that the wine and the boys were in many cases real wine and real boys, whatever else they might plausibly be in a Sufi context, could not be dismissed as mere obtuseness. And if a poet wished to write a poem that was, simply and plainly, about a sexual partner and wine, what vocabulary was available to him apart from that which the Sufi commentators were insisting must be allegorical? How would a poem that talked about a lover and wine look if it actually *was* about a lover and wine? A further factor to take into account is that each generation tends to read back into the poetry of the past its own prejudices and presuppositions. In the fourteenth century it was still common practice to write wholly secular poems that utilized vocabulary which in a Sufi poem would be designated as symbolic. In this book, many of Jahan Khatun's poems, which contain virtually no trace of any serious interest in Sufism (though she jokes about it a couple of times), are examples of this practice. But by the sixteenth century it was understood that virtually all ghazals were to be understood in Sufi, or at least nebulously mystical, terms; virtually every secular reference could be taken as allegorical, symbolic of a "mystical" meaning. Once this became the case, it was all but inevitable that earlier ghazals, such as those written by the three poets in this book, were read in these terms whenever possible.

Persian medieval lyric poetry is, then, often profoundly, and deliberately, ambiguous. An apparent "he" in a poem might equally well signify a "she" or "He." A poem might address a lover, or a patron, or God, or some combination of these three, and occasionally some other entity altogether. A reference to wine or a lover might be just that, but it might also be part of an allegory of Sufi aspiration towards the divine. Naturally, some poets avail themselves of these strategies of ambiguity more than others. Of the three poets represented in this book Obayd-e Zakani is the most direct and straightforward; the reader very rarely feels unsure of what is being talked about – what you see is more or less what you get. Jahan Malek Khatun draws on the ambiguous possibilities of medieval Persian lyrical rhetoric more than Obayd does, but she too tends to say one thing at a time, and only rarely seems to be asking her reader to consider alternative interpretations. Hafez is the Persian poet who more than any other constantly suggests multiple and shifting possibilities of meaning. This is certainly one of the reasons for his immense reputation, since his poems can be read – perfectly legitimately – in a number of ways, and this has in effect made him, in the Persian-speaking world, the poet who comes closest to being all things to all readers.

Despite the fact that by the time of his death Hafez's poems had become famous far beyond their author's hometown, very little is known about his life. Its course seems to have been fairly uneventful, in so far as the life of anyone living through such turbulent times in such a repeatedly contested city could be said to be uneventful. He was born in Shiraz, probably in 1315 (though as late as 1325 has also been suggested), and died in the same city in 1389 or 1390. To get some sense of his life, it's important to realize what a small city Shiraz was at this time; the town itself probably housed about 60,000 people, and the whole area of which it was the center had a population of perhaps 200,000. Among these 60,000 there was a high concentration of revered religious figures, and there were also many poets; it's clear that the two groups didn't always get along very well. Shiraz also had something of a reputation for debauchery, at least among some sections of the population. It was not a monoglot city: the majority spoke Persian, of which there was also a local dialect which had its own poetry, and there were Turkish and Arabic speakers, as well as speakers of Lori, the dialect of western Persia. Nor was it a city of one religion: the great majority were Sunni Moslems, but there were also Jewish and Christian inhabitants, and if Hafez is to be believed there was a Zoroastrian community there too (though it has been suggested that Hafez's Zoroastrians are more of a nostalgic fantasy than anything else – a way of saying "very Persian, but very heterodox"). As a center of trade, Shiraz had a flourishing bazaar, whose members often took to the streets during political upheavals. So although the city was small, it was also very volatile and varied, in language, religion, and ways of life. It was comparatively wealthy too (partly from its trading advantages, partly from having been spared the Mongol conquest which had devastated northern Iran), and so able to support a relatively rich court life; but this very wealth attracted trouble from outsiders who wished to get their hands on it. And lastly, Shiraz was famous for the purity of its air and the beauty of its gardens and rural surroundings; indeed, no other Persian city has inspired its poets to produce such eloquent and affectionate tributes to its charm.

In his poems Hafez praises the kings of the Inju dynasty, and he is particularly grateful to his patron the Inju king Abu Es'haq, whom he lauds for his generosity, and for the splendor of his court, with which he was clearly familiar. Soon after the Injus were overthrown by the Mozaffarid warlord Mobarez al-din in 1353, Hafez probably left the city, and he may have gone to Baghdad where the Jalayerid prince Sultan Ovays ruled (he mentions this possibility in one of his poems). In 1358, when Mobarez al-din's son, Shah Shoja, deposed his father, Hafez returned to Shiraz, and became associated with his court. Like Abu Es'haq, Shah Shoja seems to have taken a keen interest in his poets, and there is an account (by Khandamir, the same historian who related the incidents illustrating the brutality of Mobarez al-din) of him discussing Hafez's poems with their author. We know that at some point in his life Hafez visited Isfahan, as he mentions the river there, and a particular part of the city, with fond nostalgia. By the time that he died, Hafez was the most famous poet in Persia, and his fame had spread to Central Asia and India.

Despite what seems to have been their almost immediate popularity, many of Hafez's poems are not at all transparent in their meaning. It's often hard enough simply to understand what a line means, quite literally. Once this has been established there can be other problems. For instance, how does a particular line relate to the lines immediately before and after it? The difficulty of working out how the lines of Hafez's ghazals connect with one another is said to have been something about which Shah Shoja personally complained to the poet. And then, is the literal meaning the only meaning, or is there an underlying allegorical one? If both literal and allegorical meanings are present, which should we consider to be the primary one, the one carrying the narrative of the poem? Hafez's poems are packed and dense, with, as Keats says, every rift loaded with ore. It's perhaps significant that, in a culture in which poets prided themselves on their fecundity, and the facility with which they produced verse, Hafez's *Divan* ("Complete Poems") is a relatively small volume (although still fairly large compared with the collected works of many European lyric poets).[4] It's estimated that he wrote about ten poems a year, a tiny number compared with the output of most of his colleagues; clearly he revised and polished extensively,

---

4. Hafez's Divan contains 486 ghazals, and only a fairly small number of other poems. Most writers of ghazals wrote more than this (to take an extreme example, Rumi's ghazals number over 3,500), and they also tended to write long poems in other forms as well (Rumi's major work, for example, is his long narrative poem, the *Masnavi,* in six volumes). Rumi's prolixity is extraordinary even by the standards of Persian poetry, but for a major Persian poet, Hafez's oeuvre is almost equally extraordinary in the other direction, for its comparative terseness.

and the density and frequent obscurity of his verse would seem to be deliberate.[5] Two hundred years after Hafez's death, in the course of his eulogy at the grave of Torquato Tasso, Lorenzo Giacomini commented how the great Italian poet had, "avoided that superfluous facility of being at once understood, and . . . chose the novel, the unfamiliar, the unexpected, the admirable, both in ideas and in words." Giacomini meant this as high praise, and if he could have read Hafez's verse he would have recognized a kindred spirit, someone who, like Tasso, cherished complexity and "the unfamiliar, the unexpected."

The fact that Hafez "avoided that superfluous facility of being at once understood" meant that his poetry very quickly attracted commentaries. One of the first, written within two generations of Hafez's death, and certainly the most celebrated, was that by the Turkish commentator Sudi. Sudi was born in Bosnia (an indication of how far Hafez's fame had spread), which was then part of the Ottoman Empire. He was a brilliant polymath from a small village, a local boy who made good; it's likely that Persian was his third or fourth language. His commentary, which is a tour de force, is in Turkish; it was written for an audience for whom knowing Persian would be an accomplishment, something they had learned rather than imbibed with their mother's milk. The fact that it was written for such an audience has had one immense advantage for subsequent generations; Sudi explains virtually *everything* – every

---

5. This obscurity was probably a contributory factor in the elaboration of the mystical interpretation of Hafez's ghazals; if a poem didn't, at first sight, make sense in an obvious literal way, perhaps it did so in a secret, allegorical one.

word, every grammatical point, every nuance that he can detect. His temporal proximity to Hafez, and his exhaustive thoroughness, have together given his commentary great authority; but later exegetes of Hafez's work tended to see Sudi's interpretations and paraphrases as a starting point for further elaboration rather than as a definitive guide to what the poet is saying. In his commentary, Sudi tends to stick to fairly literal meanings, and when he occasionally suggests mystical or spiritual interpretations this is usually warranted in an obvious way by the vocabulary of the particular poem on which he is commenting – by, for example, a reference to "angels," or "paradise," or something similar. But subsequent commentators greatly expanded the number of Hafez's poems that were interpreted as mystical/Sufi in orientation until virtually all of them were treated in this way, and the predominantly mystical interpretation of his poetry became the standard one.

In general, the further we get from Hafez's own time the more insistent the commentators become that mystical rather than secular concerns are what the poems are "really" about. But almost from the beginning, it seems, Hafez was a revered figure, and even Sudi, for all his usual adherence to the literal implications of Hafez's vocabulary, is at pains to defend him against charges of triviality or boorishness. For example, at the end of the poem translated on pp. 82–3, Hafez says that he is "ignorant," and Sudi's comment is that this is meant satirically, as a self-deprecating joke, not literally; and then he acidly adds that anyone who concludes from this line that Hafez was ignorant has come to an ignorant conclusion. The desire to preserve Hafez's reputation from anything remotely reprehensible became standard in later commentaries, and activities such as drinking wine or flirting with pretty wine-servers, which were considered to be unworthy of so important a poet, were routinely explained away as mystical metaphors. Only in the twentieth century was this systematically mystical reading seriously challenged, and then only by a minority of critics and literary historians.

Advocates of the exclusively mystical and Sufi interpretation of Hafez's verse ("wine" in the poems means mystical doctrine or practice, which brings about the "intoxication" of mystical experience; the "friend" means God; "absence" means absence from the divine; the "wine-shop" means a Sufi meeting place, and so on) must contend with some strong contrary evidence within the poems themselves. Firstly, and very obviously, almost every time that Hafez mentions Sufis, or anything to do with Sufism, he does so with contempt. The great sin for Hafez is hypocrisy, and, as he frequently indicates, he considers Sufis to be just one more kind of hypocrite. It's been said that Hafez is deliberately leading the uninitiated astray here, or inviting contempt because the world's contempt was something that Sufis sought, but many readers will find it hard not to take him at his word. It's true that quite often Hafez indicates that he has worn the distinctive Sufi cloak himself, but when he says this he also indicates that he wasn't much of a Sufi underneath the cloak (as he believes many others who make a show of Sufism aren't either), and that the best thing to do is to shrug off the cloak. If at some point in his life he had been involved with Sufism, he seems to have thought better of it by the time that most of his poems were written.

Then there is the problem of wine in his verse. Hafez has a number of poems complaining about the closing of the wine-shops by Mobarez al-din, and other poems celebrating their reopening by Mobarez al-din's son, Shah Shoja. It's hard to see how the wine in these poems could be anything other than real. This is not to say that the wine in his poems can never have Sufi implications, since Hafez often appears to be playing with this possibility (playing with possibilities is a mode in which Hafez seems to be particularly at home), but my own feeling is that the wine in his poems is usually just that, literal wine. There is also the tone of Hafez's lyrics to consider, especially when we compare them with lyrics by self-proclaimed Sufis or Sufi sympathizers such as Eraqi, Attar, or Rumi. The tone in these poets' lyrical works tends to be consistent, focused, often relentless in its concentration; this is true of very few of Hafez's poems, which tend to shift abruptly in tone and register, and can draw on quite different areas of knowledge or experience within just a few lines. Hafez's poems often seem to seek to undermine any sense that there is one truth to be pursued at the cost of all others (which is of course the central tenet of Sufi poetry); his verse frequently slips or swerves from possibility to possibility in a way that is quite untypical of most unequivocally Sufi verse in Persian.

The assumption that Hafez's poems must be about more serious things than drinking wine and flirting with pretty wine-servers may derive, to some extent, from the accepted explanation of his pen-name, Hafez (his given name was Shams al-din Mohammad; like most Persian poets, he wrote under a pseudonym). It's pointed out that

"Hafez" means "One who knows the Qur'an by heart," and by extension "One who recites the Qur'an." The word comes from an Arabic root that means "to preserve" or "to keep," and a *hafez* is someone who preserves the Qur'an in his heart. To give so much attention to flirting and wine-drinking seems more than a little inappropriate for someone who is publicly announcing that he knows the Qur'an by heart. But *hafez* also had another meaning in medieval Persian, according to which what was preserved in the heart was not the Qur'an but a knowledge of musical technique (which was passed on entirely by example and apprenticeship, not by texts, so music needed such "preservers" if it was to survive from one generation to the next). In medieval Iran "Hafez" was a fairly common soubriquet for a professional musician, especially a singer (the Iranian writer Homa Nateq lists a number of medieval musicians who incorporated the word *hafez* into their performing name, as a kind of advertisement of their musical mastery[6]). Musicians in medieval Persian society suggested almost exactly the opposite of what would be suggested by a reciter of the Qur'an, which was necessarily a respectable profession that presupposed a sober disposition. Musicians, on the other hand, were considered to be a fairly disreputable bunch, associated with dissipated and sometimes riotous behavior, a lifestyle that to the religiously respectable would be considered immoral.

On the other hand, some of Hafez's poems are undoubtedly about serious concerns that might be

---

6. Homa Nateq, *Hafez: khonyagari, may o shadi* (Los Angeles: Ketab Corporation, 2004), pp. 61–79.

designated religious. More than once he says he is a bird from paradise trapped in the world, and that he wishes to return to a paradisal state. His mind is nagged by the unknowableness of life's purposes, and he sometimes wonders whether it has a purpose at all. His verse is full of imagery and individuals drawn from religious tradition, and he talks about God's forgiveness (of which he usually says he feels assured, despite the condemnation by others of the dissipated way in which he lives). His religious feelings are strong but unspecific, and he insists that they cross the boundaries of particular faiths; he says that Moslems, Christians, and Jews have an equal purchase on truth, but that love and compassion are the best guides to conduct, since dogmatic knowledge is unattainable. He doesn't know, and he says no one else can know either, but he quests and searches.

So does this mean that the religious, Qur'anic, meaning of *hafez* is, after all, the right one in his case? Possibly. But when we consider the jarring dichotomies within his poems, it seems most useful to recognize both meanings as being invoked by his pen-name: the lofty and religious on the one hand, and the dissipated and secular on the other. It's even plausible that the presence of these two meanings, with their contradictory connotations, was precisely the reason that he chose "Hafez" as his pen-name. The name is a constant pun, one that evokes both the serious and the scandalous, the exaltedly religious and the sexily secular, that moves between both worlds, as Hafez's poems do. To a medieval audience, the name would also have invoked the idea of music; it's clear from his poems that Hafez loved music, and in his commentary Sudi remarks that Hafez was famous for the sweetness of his singing voice. It's virtually certain that his poems were meant to be sung as much as to be recited, and that their association with musical performance (which still continues) was a strong one from the time that they were written.

While it's difficult to characterize Hafez in terms of western parallels, relating him to figures from European literature might be helpful to Anglophone readers. He can seem at times like Horace, in his simultaneous and paradoxical dependence on munificent patronage while advocating the joys of privacy and friendship away from centers of power; a love of wine and a ruefully acknowledged susceptibility to the pleasures and pains of Eros also unite them. He can seem like the medieval troubadours of southern Europe in his linking of poetry and music, and in the way that his verse is undoubtedly courtly and written for members of courts, but also has clear suggestions of a vagabond disreputableness about it. He can sound especially like those troubadours who practiced *trobar clus* ("closed form"), a style of verse deliberately packed with difficulties and allusions likely to be lost on outsiders – a technique which was, as Hafez says in one of his rubaiyat,[7] meant for "art's initiates," excluding those not in the know. He can seem like Shakespeare in his abrupt switches of tone and scope of reference, the way wholly disparate areas of human experience are drawn into the same poetic moment. If we jump forward in time to a poet of a very different kind, Hafez's poems can remind us of the songs of Bob Dylan, particularly his more meditative

7. Rubai (plural rubaiyat): a four-line epigrammatic poem, usually rhyming *aaba*, sometimes *aaaa*.

ones. Again, there is the music, and also the way a Dylan song often hovers at the edge of the paraphrasable, which might be because we don't have enough background information to attempt the paraphrase, or because there isn't a paraphrase, a back-story, to be found at all, simply a series of images that create a pervasive mood and suggest a thematic coherence. There is too the loathing of hypocrisy that comes through in some of Dylan's songs, the earnest sense, casually conveyed, that life is too serious for posturing and lies. "So let us not speak falsely now, the hour is getting late" could easily be a line from Hafez.

Jahan Malek Khatun

Hafez is among the two or three most famous Persian poets who have ever lived. Until quite recently, virtually no one had heard of Jahan Khatun. She had been known, locally at least, as a poet in her own lifetime, and after her death a few historians and retailers of literary anecdotes mentioned her, usually in passing, but to all intents and purposes she disappeared from view until her complete poems, in a bulky volume of over 550 pages, received their first publication in 1995. To have this extraordinary poet's fascinating and often very beautiful poems emerge from six hundred years of virtual oblivion seems almost miraculous.

Jahan Khatun's parents married in 1324, and it seems that Jahan was their only child. She herself married at some time between 1343 and 1347; assuming that 1325 is the earliest she could have been born, she would have been in her early twenties, or (more probably) her teens at the time of her marriage. Her father, Masud Shah, king of Shiraz and Fars from 1336 to 1339, was murdered in 1342, soon after he had tried to take back the throne. Jahan Khatun cannot have been more than seventeen at the time of her father's death, and she was probably a few years younger than this. Her uncle, Abu Es'haq, who became king in 1343, looked after her, and she became a cherished member of his court. As we have seen, Abu Es'haq was famous for his love of poetry and his patronage of poets (including Hafez and Obayd-e Zakani) and it is very likely that he encouraged Jahan to write, despite the fact that it was at this time relatively unusual, though not unprecedented, for women to write poetry (or at least to write poetry that was circulated beyond an immediate circle of friends). One reason for this is that such an activity was thought to be immodest, and women tended not to be taught to read and write.[8] Jahan was a notable exception: literate from a young age, she was also clearly quite capable of deciding for herself how much modesty she needed to display. It also seems more than plausible that, given Jahan's dependence on her uncle and what we can imagine would be her feelings of gratitude toward him, she took up poetry partly as a way

---

8. Writing was considered to belong to the world of public affairs, and also to be an intellectual accomplishment – women were considered to be "private" citizens who had no business in public affairs, as well as being intrinsically without intellectual potential. Another basic, perhaps subconscious, reason for illiteracy among women may be that access to reading and writing confers relative autonomy: once you can read and write, you can communicate with those who are absent/elsewhere – they can speak to you and you can speak to them – and, given the nature of society in Jahan's time, this was out of the question for most women.

of pleasing him, as there were few surer ways of giving Abu Es'haq pleasure than writing him a good poem.

The man she married was her uncle's *nadim* – his bosom-buddy, drinking companion, and confidant – Amin al-din Jahromi. Whether this was in any way a love match we have no way of knowing. Certainly, whether or not mutual affection was involved, it will have been largely an arranged marriage. If Abu Es'haq had said, "You two should marry one another," it would have been virtually unthinkable for either of them to say in response, "I'd rather not."

The great majority of Jahan Khatun's poems are love poems, and they are usually about unhappiness in love. This is standard for lyric poets of her time, and nothing can be read into it. Indeed, taking a medieval poet's poems as evidence of his or her life is an extremely risky thing to do. But one or two hints are perhaps significant. For example, as Abu Es'haq's drinking companion, Amin al-din Jahromi was expected to stay up all night drinking with the king when this was what the king wished. More than once Jahan Khatun says that she doesn't like a lover who is drunk; this is distinctive – it's not a common trope in the poetry of the time. More than once, too, she says she lies awake all night waiting for her lover, who is off drinking somewhere, to come to her; or she mentions the fact that, when they share a bed, he's in a drunken stupor, and she doesn't like this either. In one poem she seems to refer to the marriage vows as the only time she has ever heard her lover say "yes" to her (see p. 175). But then a number of her poems also refer to happiness in love, occasionally in the present, more often as something from the past that is now remembered with affectionate nostalgia.

Did she have other lovers besides her husband? Some of her poems seem to imply this, or at least to suggest that she has been in love with more than one person. To have taken a lover would have been very risky, if perhaps a bit less perilous for a favored princess than for most other women. There is some evidence that she married twice – two different possible husbands are referred to in biographical notices about her – though whether this was as the result of a divorce or her first husband's death is unclear. The biographical notices also say she was extremely beautiful. The few female poets of medieval Iran are virtually always described in this way, but then they would be, wouldn't they? Perhaps, though, she was indeed very beautiful; she certainly attracted notice, admiration, and envy. Some of her poems seem to indicate that she herself thought she was beautiful; this again is not a standard trope in the poetry of the period (boasting in medieval Persian poems is common enough, but it's usually about one's poetic abilities, rather than one's physical charms), and so perhaps it indicates something she genuinely believed about herself, or at least something a lot of people had told her. At some point in her life Jahan Khatun had a daughter who died while still an infant or very young child; the grief apparent in the poems that she wrote in her daughter's memory (there are twenty-three of them in all, varying from the longest, consisting of thirty-one double lines – what in English would be considered as sixty-two lines – to a number of four-line poems) is very affecting, and is obviously genuine.

The palmy days of being a pampered princess at the center of a poetry-loving court did not last long, however. In 1353 Mobarez al-din marched an army out from Kerman, where he had his base, defeated Jahan Khatun's uncle on the battlefield, and took over the government of Shiraz. In 1357 her uncle was brought back from Isfahan, where he had taken refuge, and executed. What happened to Jahan Khatun in the immediate aftermath is unclear, but for a while her life must have been in real danger. One poem, significantly enough written in the "fragment" (*qate'*) form, which was often used for personal anecdote and reminiscence, describes her as being held prisoner in a school while her captors argue as to what should be done with her (see p. 182). Another poem mentions the fact that, while she was imprisoned, no one at court dared mention her name (see p. 189). Still other poems, some of them again in the personal *qate'* form, imply that she was forced into exile. Capture, imprisonment, and then exile seem to have been her fate; such a sequence of events seems more than plausible, but again we have to remember how unreliable medieval poetry can be as a source for autobiography, and no other sources mention what happened to her at this period in her life. It's possible too that her husband, as one of Abu Es'haq's closest associates, had shared the same fate as his prince, which would have meant that Jahan Khatun was now a widow. Certainly in the poems about exile it sounds as though she is really alone, with no one in whom she can confide. Perhaps it was at this point that she turned to religion; in a number of her poems she indicates that, as the world has treated her so wretchedly, she will now put her faith in God alone, not in her fellow men and women. The trope is conventional enough, but it fits her probable circumstances, and these poems can have the ring of bitterness and belief, of a personal disillusionment with the world.

Events took a turn for the better for Jahan Khatun five years after Mobarez al-din had become the ruler of Shiraz, when his son Shah Shoja deposed him. Shah Shoja seems to have gone out of his way not only to reverse his father's austerely ascetic public policies, but also to make friendly overtures to the poets whom his father had alienated. Like Abu Es'haq, he made his court a center of poetic activity, though one gets the impression that he was more of a fairly generous, hale-fellow-well-met kind of a ruler than the connoisseur and crony of poets that Abu Es'haq had been. On the plus side, he was politically astute where Abu Es'haq had been self-indulgent to the point of incompetence, and for most of the time his reign was a much more secure affair than Abu Es'haq's had ever been. If Jahan Khatun was living in exile when Shah Shoja replaced his father as king, she returned to Shiraz soon after this, and seems to have remained there until her death. Whether she actually became a member of Shah Shoja's court or not is not known, but she wrote poems in his praise, and seems to have been allowed to live out her days unmolested and in reasonable dignity. Her last poem dateable by internal evidence (a reference to Shah Shoja's briefly reigning nephew) seems to have been written around 1393, by which time she will have been in her mid or late sixties; when she died is unknown.

Jahan Khatun's *Divan* ("Complete Poems") is quite substantial, as it contains 1,413 ghazals (three times as many as Hafez's *Divan*), the above-mentioned elegies for her daughter, over 300 rubaiyat, four praise poems (some of her ghazals are also, in effect, praise poems), and various fragments. It also contains a prose preface, written by herself, about her poems. While this is unique among the surviving works of Persian woman poets from the medieval period, it is frustratingly short on specific information both about her life and the circumstances in which her poems were written. Presumably she personally prepared the manuscript for copying, nevertheless the copies seem to be in a somewhat tentative state. For example, in a number of cases ghazals listed as separate poems look like drafts of the same poem, as they contain some of the same lines and rhymes juggled about in a different order. Four copies of the manuscript are known to have survived, two complete (and thought to have been copied either in her own lifetime or very shortly after her death), and two fragmentary – we can compare this with the, for example, over one thousand known manuscripts of Hafez's poems.

Even if their quality were fairly negligible (which is far from being the case), Jahan Khatun's poems would be of interest simply because hers is the only complete collection by a woman writing in Persian, at a time when it was considered anomalous for women to write poetry, to have come down to us from before the nineteenth century. Her preface may not give much away about her life, but it does touch on her ambitions as a poet. She had wanted to write poetry for some time (and she is eloquent as to why – as a stay against oblivion, as a comfort in her solitude), and had begun to do so, but she was held back by two things. Firstly she felt that this was perhaps not a suitable occupation for a woman, and secondly she was not sure she had sufficient talent to consider herself a "real" poet. She asks her readers to excuse her faults; as she modestly puts it:

> Not every eye can gaze at the sun
> Not every drop can reach the sea

However, she was encouraged by the fact that various other women had written poetry before her in both Arabic and Persian (she lists a number of such poets by name), so she thought it would be allowable for her to do this too.

Most of Jahan Khatun's poems are ghazals, and, as we have seen, the rhetoric of the ghazal had been elaborated for a particular kind of poem, one supposedly written by an adult male to a younger lover who is in most cases considered to be a male adolescent. There is a paradoxical fiction at the heart of the ghazal: the rhetoric of the poem is that the speaker is inferior to the addressee, but in so far as these poems reflected any sort of social reality, the speaker was virtually always superior to the addressee – an older person, usually more powerful and wealthy, while the addressee was often a servant or a slave. When a woman uses such rhetoric some peculiar tensions are immediately set up: is she writing as a woman or is she writing as a man, and, if the latter, is this done with or without irony? And who is she writing to? Is this still basically a homoerotic poem, or can it now be assumed to be heterosexual, with the addressee to be considered as male? And is the addressee still a younger person, a pretty adolescent? Or, now that a woman is writing, should we consider the addressee to be a man of the same age, or perhaps older? The ironies are compounded by the fact that it is not only a woman writing but a princess. How seriously can we take a princess when she presents herself as inferior to the addressee of her poem?

One way of solving, or at least sidestepping, these questions, is to say that Jahan Khatun simply observes the conventions of writing as if she were male, and that the poems are to be taken as exercises within a given genre. In other words, the author's gender should be neither here nor there when the poems are considered as examples of the particular genre to which they belong. This is true, up to a point.

It's certainly the case that Jahan Khatun usually writes "as" a male (and, which can be something of a break with the usual conventions of the ghazal, sometimes as a male apparently addressing a woman). That she is clearly writing from within male conventions is shown by the fact that she will use tropes natural to a male writer, but which can cause a readerly double-take coming from a female one. For example, she will ask people not to pluck at her beard (that is, deride her or tease her), or she will ask her lover not to veil him(?) self before her. Neither of these conventions makes literal sense spoken by a woman to a man. (A contemporary reader might possibly think that when she asks her lover not to veil herself, she is in reality talking to a woman, and that perhaps Jahan Khatun liked girls, but women didn't veil themselves before other women, and the trope still makes no literal sense.) This means that she is using the tropes for their tenor (what they actually mean) rather than for the vehicle/metaphor that conveys the tenor: "don't pluck at my beard" means "don't bother me"; "don't veil yourself from me" means "don't disappear and leave me." In one ghazal she invokes a number of pairs of legendary pre-Islamic lovers, always casting herself as the male, the addressee as the female:[9]

> You are Layla, you are Layla . . .
> I am Majnun, I am Majnun, I am Majnun . . .
> You are Shirin . . .
> I am Farhad . . .
> You are Shirin, you are Shirin, you are Shirin. . .
> I am Khosrow . . .
> You are Azra, you are Azra . . .
> I am Vameq, I am Vameq . . .
> You are Golshah, you are Golshah . . .
> I am Varqeh, I am Varqeh . . .
> You are Vis . . .
> I am Ramin . . .

But the fact that she is in reality a woman, and that her audience would know this, frequently tweaks the poetic conventions, and much of the piquancy in her poems comes from this disjunction between what we as readers know about the author (that she was a woman, something her original audience of course also knew) and the "male" assumptions inherent in the genre in which she is writing. At such moments we have glimpses of the kind of complex, self-mirroring eroticism that happens in Shakespearian

---

9. In one rubai, she does however refer to herself as "like Layla" – that is, as the woman of the pair – and her lover as Majnun, the man, though this identification of herself with a feminine heroine from the past is rare.

comedy, when boys pretending to be girls dress up as boys, which everyone knows they "really" are in the world outside the theatre, while remaining as "really" girls for as long as the play lasts. Jahan Khatun is really a woman, but for as long as the poem lasts, she is doing what a man does and assuming a male persona, and as that fictive man she can, as male poets do, assume traditionally inferior – that is "feminine" – roles (of submissiveness, begging, flirtation, midnight tears, and so on). As previously stated, the paradox of assumed submissiveness for the male writer of the ghazal is that the speaker is in fact almost always more socially powerful than the addressee, who is often a young servant or slave. Jahan Khatun, by the sheer fact of her sex, eroticizes, or more accurately "genderizes," this social disparity. And there is a further twist: as a princess she is superior to almost anyone she might address, but as a woman she is, in the gender terms of her social milieu, inferior to almost any male lover she might address. Her poems play with these paradoxes constantly, and the reader often glimpses her appearing to get a heady kick out of the game. Despite the extreme conventionality of the rhetoric and situations of her ghazals, their tone is often distinctive and memorable; this is in large part due, I think, to the ambiguity – almost duplicity – of the gender (and to a lesser extent social) roles in them. The issue of gender is a tense one in her poems, and she uses that tension to express tension about other things, such as social hierarchy and politics. Once the reader is attuned to this gender ambiguity and to the delicate interplay of power and powerlessness – the ways in which the conventions of the poetic tradition within which she is writing, her gender, and her social status all meld and confirm and contradict one another in her poems – getting to know her oeuvre can be an extraordinarily subtle and moving experience. Another distinctive quality of her verse is that she can be both plangent and flippant in the same poem, sometimes in the same thought, a quality that can probably be traced back at least in part to a consciousness of the ambiguous gender and social status that she assumes in any given poem.

The fundamental and most common theme of her poetry is a sense of lost happiness, and given her history it is easy to see why this should be the case (the murder of her father when she was in her teens would probably have been enough to set her off on such a course, quite apart from everything that happened to her subsequently). What is so notable is the way that she can use the conventions of the love poem, in which the theme of lost happiness was considered natural and expected, to parley this general apprehension into poems about politics and social upheaval – the rhetoric and the emotional tenor are continuous, although the subjects she brings them to could hardly be more different from one another. But we should remember that this pervasive sadness is not her only tone: she can joke with her lover(s) too, and she can be light-heartedly excited at times, especially in her evocations of outdoor social gatherings. Like Hafez, she seems to have had a special love of music, particularly the music that accompanied poetry. In one of her ghazals she says,

If you get hold of Jahan's poems
Take up an instrument to pass the time,
And sing one or two of her lines with a sweet voice;
Let the sounds of the tambourine and flute delight you . . .

It is instructive to compare the poetry of Hafez and Jahan Khatun to see how what are basically the same conventions, the same metaphors, and the same rhetorical tropes, can produce poems that speak to us with such distinctly disparate, individual voices. Within the same deployed conventions of the ghazal, we can discern distinct psychological profiles, or at least stylistic emphases that can suggest psychological leanings beneath them. Hafez loves to imply a number of things at once; Jahan Khatun tends to say one thing at a time. Sufi notions hover around – many would say wholly pervade – a number of Hafez's poems; Jahan Khatun almost never mentions Sufism. Jahan Khatun is a more plaintive and direct writer than Hafez; Hafez is a more dismissive and evasive writer than Jahan Khatun. He is also much more Anacreontic, bibulous, crapulous, and generally wine-besotted than Jahan Khatun, who mentions wine according to the usual conventions but rarely dwells on it, and who more than once indicates that she doesn't much like it when her lover(s) are drunk. Jahan Khatun's tone, except when she is angry about politics, is almost always elegant and appropriately aristocratic; we feel she's a very well-brought-up young lady, if also one who has sometimes been ready to kick over the traces erotically (at least imaginatively, possibly actually). Hafez's tone is far more various and capricious; it's the tone of someone who doesn't have a respectable public persona to keep up; of someone, in fact, whose public persona is that he *isn't* respectable. We can perhaps glimpse a particular difference in these two authors' sense of themselves *as poets* in their treatment of the convention that the author's pen-name should appear in a ghazal's closing lines. It was common for poets to boast about their poetic prowess at this moment (such poetic self-promotion had a particular name, *fakr*), and Hafez very often does this, announcing in effect that no better poet than himself can be found anywhere. Jahan Khatun almost never boasts in this way; instead she often puns on her name, Jahan, which means "world." This too might seem grandiose, like Hafez's *fakr*, but in reality the pun almost always diminishes her; it talks about a lost world, or a broken world, or a world upset, imprisoned, or in tears. The very fact that she puns on her name so often as her poems end, as if her identity is in doubt or dissolving into something else, seems indicative of her fluctuating sense of self.

It is often when poets who write largely within a stylized set of expectations innovate that we feel we come closest to their preoccupations and personalities. Hafez's vehemence against religious hypocrisy is one of his greatest themes, and he was virtually the first poet to give it such constant emphasis; here, we are convinced, is something dear to his heart. Jahan Khatun's most obvious departure from convention is that, though she often appears to speak in her poetic voice "as a man," her ghazals are fairly unequivocally heterosexual in their implications. A further distinctive feature of her poetry is her use of the rhetoric of hopeless love to comment on her hopeless political situation, after her immediate family lost power in Shiraz, and this too seems to bring us closer to her as a person, rather than simply as a skilled manipulator of language. If we must always remember that these poems are above all exercises in style, we can also invoke Buffon's aphorism "*Le style, c'est l'homme même*" ("Style is the man himself"). The style is a fashion that everyone wears (everyone uses more or less the same conventions when he/she writes a ghazal), but the reader who becomes intimate with the fashion can discern distinctive traits that point to the personal preoccupations, predilections, and foibles of the wearer. And some people just do it so well that you feel a fundamental part of the personality is a flair and élan that lift them effortlessly above the crowd. For all their differences, Hafez and Jahan Khatun share this quality.

It is indicative, too, to see how these two poets built on and reacted to the inheritance of their great poetic predecessor in Shiraz, Sa'di. Sa'di had been born into a world that was much more coherent and cohesive culturally than that of his fourteenth-century successors, but the second half of his life was passed in as troubled times as theirs. His major work, the *Golestan* ("The Rose Garden"), was written in 1258, the year of the sack of Baghdad by the Mongols, and the subsequent destruction of the Abbasid caliphate, which had ruled most of the Islamic world since the eighth century. Sa'di's poetry was seen as exemplifying a previously unattained purity of form and sentiment. Formally, his verses were characterized by what was called his "difficult simplicity," a sophisticated limpidity of language that appeared guileless and easy, but which was thought to be almost inimitable. His sentiments advocated an easygoing humane tolerance, which was taken as the mark of a noble and generous poetic nature. They are well typified by his verses now inscribed in the main hall of the United Nations Building:

> Man's sons are parts of one reality
> Since all have sprung from one identity;
> If one part of a body's hurt, the rest
> Cannot remain unmoved and undistressed;
> If you're not touched by others' pain, the name
> Of "man" is one you cannot rightly claim.

In a way, Jahan Khatun and Hafez can be said to have divided up, and internalized and intensified, Sa'di's legacy between them. Jahan Khatun's poems sometimes echo phrases by the Shirazi poet Khaju, and occasionally moments in her verse will seem to allude to comparable moments in Hafez's poems, but her most obvious stylistic debt, one she acknowledges, is to Sa'di. She consciously strives for his clarity and elegance, and her poems are often similar to his, both in the tropes they typically utilize and in the way they can at their best suggest a kind of distilled essence of pure lyric feeling. But Jahan Khatun's verse also takes Sa'di's achievement in a particular direction. For all the conventionality of their language, her poems suggest the inwardness of a specific individual sensibility; they use generic, conventional means to produce a distinctively personal voice. Hafez complicates and expands the legacy he receives from Sa'di; no one could accuse his poems of "simplicity," obscure or otherwise, and Sa'di's tolerance is taken by Hafez in directions the thirteenth-century poet could not have foreseen and perhaps would not have countenanced. It's clear from both his prose works and his poems that Sa'di's much vaunted tolerance tended to stop short at the boundaries of Islam; Hafez's emphatically does not. And like Jahan Khatun, Hafez personalizes his inheritance from his great predecessor: if Sa'di very often seems to be saying in quietly deprecating tones, "Don't be censorious, leave others alone," Hafez equally often brings the sentiment abruptly home by saying in effect, "Don't be censorious, leave *me* alone."

Obayd-e Zakani

There is an interesting, rather eccentric Shirazi poet of a slightly later generation than the poets in this book (assumed to have been born in the mid fourteenth century, he died in 1427), Sheikh Bos'haq At`ameh Halaj Shirazi, commonly known simply as Bos'haq. He is often linked with Obayd, because both of them dealt with mundane or even sordid things, in a mock-heroic manner, and Bos'haq acknowledges his debt to the earlier poet. Bos'haq's specialty was writing about food and recipes (the word "At`ameh" in his name means "edibles"). Frequently his poems were gastronomic parodies of "classic" poems, as though an English-speaking poet might write a culinary poem parodying a well-known Shakespeare sonnet:

> Shall I compare thee to a lamb kebab?
> Thou art more tasty and more temperate . . .

Bos'haq parodies a number of poems by Hafez in this way. Take, for example, the poem on pp. 98–9, which begins:

> A loving friend, good wine, a place secure
> From enemies –
> What luck is yours if you can always lay
> Your hands on these!

Bos'haq's parody of this begins:

> A loving friend, good saffron rice,
>   With oil inside it –
> What luck is yours, if there should be
>   Halva beside it!

In bracketing himself with Obayd, Bos'haq pays the older poet a rather back-handed tribute:

> Imagine that each poet has contributed with his verses to the building of a house, but one that had neither a privy nor a kitchen. My master Obayd has built the privy, and your humble servant has built the kitchen. From his verses comes the smell of someone loosening his underwear, from mine the fragrance of a cloth spread with good things to eat.[10]

It is as Persian literature's prime "privy/lavatorial" poet that Obayd-e Zakani is best known, although his range is wider than this, and he could also on occasion write charming and wholly respectable lyric poems as well as, or better than, the next poet. He wrote prose as well as poetry, and his forte is satire, which generally goes with a hatred of hypocrisy (a hatred the three poets in this book shared). Obayd's satire is often quite dirty-minded, and it's written with great gusto. He can be simultaneously coarse and learned, like Rabelais, or he can indulge in vituperation and satirical fantasy, like Swift; his complaints about his debts and his unabashed boasting about begging his way

---

10. Hosein Ma`refat (ed.), *Divan-e Molana Bos'haq Halaj-e Shirazi, Mashur be At`ameh* (Shiraz: Ketab Forushi-e Ma`refat-e Shiraz, 1320/1941), p. 181.

through life on the fringes of society can sometimes make him sound like a Persian François Villon.

Unlike Hafez, Jahan Khatun, and Bos'haq, Obayd was not born in Shiraz, but in Qazvin, in northern Iran, around 1300. The name Zakani was said to come from that of an Arab tribe from which his family claimed descent. The men of his family appear to have been career civil servants, happy to serve whichever local monarch might employ them. It's clear from Obayd's writings that he had received a good education as a young man; he might have used his learning for facetious and sometimes obscene purposes, but there was no doubt of its extent and sophistication. He moved to Shiraz at some point, perhaps attracted by reports of Abu Es'haq's liberality towards poets, and for a time was a member of his court. The constant complaints about his debts and poverty that repeatedly crop up in his poems are not unusual in the work of medieval poets, particularly itinerant ones, which Obayd was for a while, but he does seem to be especially insistent about it, which perhaps suggests that he couldn't hold any position down for long. His habitually sharp tongue, which he seems to have had difficulty controlling, might well have got him thrown out of more than one court. His poems express great affection for Shiraz, just as much as that expressed by the native-born Jahan Khatun and Hafez, but he seems not to have settled there. Not surprisingly, given his reputation for dissipation and generally appalling manners, he left town when Mobarez al-din took over, and returned to Shiraz when Shah Shoja became king. But by then he may have felt the glory days were over, or he may have fallen foul of Shah Shoja, as he seems to have been particularly good at annoying his patrons. For whatever reason, he appears to have spent his last years back in his home town of Qazvin. He died in 1370.

There is a tradition of Obayd's poetic rivalry with Jahan Khatun, and the two poems ascribed to him that are about Jahan Khatun (one has survived only as a single-line fragment) are singularly nasty. These poems appeared in a fifteenth-century work on poets, *Tazkirat al-Sho`ara* ("Memorials of the Poets"), by Amir Dowlatshah Samarqandi, and it's possible they are not by Obayd at all (they have also been attributed to the poet Kamal Khojandi, 1320–1401), but because they seem typical of Obayd's manner, and are so specific in their target, they are usually assumed to be genuine. One warns a prospective husband not to marry Jahan, and Obayd uses the habitual pun in Jahan's poems (Jahan/world) against her. Typically of Obayd's poetic technique, he takes a commonplace of the poetic tradition ("the world is faithless") and twists it to make an obscene point. His language is as bluntly unpleasant as the translation indicates:

> My lord, the world's [i.e. Jahan's] a faithless whore;
> Aren't you ashamed of this whore's fame?
> Go, seek some other cunt out – God
> Himself can't make Jahan feel shame.

The surviving line from another poem states that even if her poems should reach India, it would be quite clear that they were written by a woman (this is obviously meant as dismissive), except that he uses the same obscenity as in the previous poem instead of the word for "woman." A sixteenth-century commentator wrote that Jahan Khatun was the center of her own group of poets at the Inju court (holding what would later be called in Europe a literary salon) and that Obayd was jealous of her success and popularity, which is why he wrote so vituperatively about her. The story may have some truth in it, but it could also have been elaborated simply in order to provide a context for Obayd's poems about Jahan Khatun. If the poems are indeed by Obayd, it's very easy to see why courts quickly grew tired of his company. It also probably says something for the Inju family's tolerance that nothing further seems to have happened to him as a result of this; one can imagine a different princess demanding his head on a platter, and perhaps getting it. On the other hand, a more depressing possibility is that insults to women just didn't matter that much, even if the woman in question was a princess.

Even though it's hard for us not to feel that Obayd comes out of his quarrel with Jahan Khatun looking like a graceless lout, this should not blind us to the fact that many of his targets were much more worthy of his contempt. Like Swift he seems to have been eaten up with "savage indignation" at the venality of much of the world. His satirical prose works often have an easy-going, jokey surface but the anger keeps breaking through. One of his prose works is a kind of *Devil's Dictionary*, written long before Ambrose Bierce had the same idea, in which he provides facetious and damning definitions for words. Here are a few (slightly adapted from the admirable translation by Hasan Javadi):

> *The Man of Learning*: A man who cannot even earn his own livelihood.
>
> *The Ignorant*: Fortune's favorite.
>
> *The Judge:* A man who is cursed by everyone.
>
> *The Sufi*: A freeloader.
>
> *The Aphrodisiac*: The leg of someone else's wife.
>
> *Virginity:* A word with no referent . . .

And he doesn't spare his own professions:

> *The Courtier*: A sycophant.
>
> *The Poet*: A greedy braggart . . .

Perhaps the most poignant definition of them all is

> *Man*: One who is not a hypocrite.[11]

Another prose work, *The Ethics of the Aristocrats*, gives similar but more lengthy definitions, this time of virtues (wisdom, courage, chastity, and so forth). In these he first sets out the "abrogated" version of each virtue, and by this he means what everyone normally understands the word in question to mean. He then says that these abrogated versions are obsolete, and goes on to describe the new version, which is the exact opposite of what the virtue is supposed to be (for example, the new version of courage is cowardice, and includes "Running away in time . . . "). The new definitions are defended with an elaborate show of specious learning, with (often genuine) quotations from religious and learned authorities to back up their travesties of meaning.

---

11. Hasan Javadi, *Obeyd-e Zakani: Ethics of the Aristocrats and Other Satirical Works* (Washington, D.C.: Mage Publishers, 2008). The quoted definitions are from pp. 63–71.

But Obayd is best known for his obscene poems, some of which have been translated for this book. Because he is so open about sexual matters, unlike virtually all his contemporaries, his evidence as to sexual mores is valuable, even if we have to take its habitual hyperbole with a good pinch of salt. Until very recently, Obayd's poems were always printed with gaps to indicate the obscene words, or with the first letter of the word followed by suspension points (which wasn't very helpful as a number of the most obscene words in Persian start with the same letter). A complete unbowdlerized text was not published until 1999, in New York; it has yet to appear in Iran. Often the reason given for this censorship was that the poems were so open about pederasty. It's true that they are, but then they are very open about heterosexuality too, and in fact Obayd has some poems that debate the relative virtues and disadvantages of male and female genitals, and of boys or girls as sexual partners.[12] He also has a long poem (not included here) in praise of masturbation; the poem is, among other things, an attack on Sufis, who he says are much given to the practice, and about whom he is even more contemptuous than Hafez manages to be.

Like many satirists, Obayd seems to see himself primarily as a truth-teller; this is borne out partly by his pen-name, which is simply a shortened form of his given name (Obaydullah). It's not an adopted, chosen name that has a special meaning, or meanings (like "Hafez"), and neither is it a part of his own name that has an especially

---

12. Interestingly enough, Ernst Curtius, op. cit., p. 116, reports that poetic debates on the same subject were written "in humanistic circles" in eleventh- and twelfth-century Europe.

resonant implication that he can make elaborate rhetorical points with (like "Jahan"). It's simply a shortened form of his given name that by itself means "servant," although he makes no great play with this fact. It's as if by adopting this very modest, almost anonymous, pen-name – almost a non pen-name, in fact – he is saying, "I'm not pretending to be anything; I'm just who I am."

Despite his fame primarily as an obscene poet, Obayd-e Zakani's single best-known poem is not concerned with sex at all, but with the politics of Shiraz and the fall of the Inju family at the hands of the Mozaffarid conqueror Mobarez al-din. This is *Cat and Mouse* (see pp. 217–23), an animal fable that tells the tale of Mobarez al-din's conquest as a kind of cautionary tale, one that might be thought to be primarily a children's story – as Swift's *Gulliver's Travels* has sometimes been considered to be – were it not for the satirical edge of Obayd's scorn for human folly. Again, we see Obayd using the rhetoric of "serious" literature in order to write something facetious and scurrilous. He parodies a number of "high" literary styles in the course of his poem, most obviously those of panegyric and epic. This kind of playing with the rhetoric of particular literary genres is, unfortunately, largely lost in translation, although a general mock-heroic tone can give a broad idea of what is going on. For both Persian and English readers alike, it must be assumed that many of Obayd's particular satirical points now pass us by unremarked, because we no longer know the individuals or circumstances to which he was referring; political satire probably has the shortest shelf-life of any literary genre. Nevertheless, the poem has retained its popularity as the most famous pre-modern verse satire in Persian, partly because of the evident zest with which the tale is told, partly because of the memorable vignettes of the argumentative, cowardly mice and the aggressive, vindictive cat, and I hope something of these characteristics comes through in the translation.

The Translations

Translating lyric poetry presents particular problems when we compare it to translating narrative or epigrammatic verse. In both the latter forms there is a verifiable out-there-in-the-world content to consider and convey: in the narrative there is the story; in the epigram there is a particular, snappily put insight about human nature. In the lyric, by contrast, the actual verifiable content can be very slight (lyrics tend to *say* a fairly small number of things, "I want you"; "You're absolutely marvelous"; "You're making me really miserable"; "You make me deliriously happy"; "Is there any hope for me?"). In so far as the interest resides in the content, it is usually to be found more in how that content is presented rather than in what the content is. But the real subject of a lyric is very often something inward, and to this extent more inapprehensible, and so harder to paraphrase than a story with heroes and incidents; the lyric deals in feeling rather than fact. What the translator finds himself trying to bring over is style and sensibility. If, at times, the feeling and form of a narrative passage elude a translator, he has at least the story to fall back on; if the feeling and form of a lyric poem elude the translator, he has, practically speaking, nothing.

This means that the form of a lyric poem is particularly important for the translator who wishes to convey at least something of what reading the poem in its original language is like. This accounts for the use of rhyme and fairly strict metrical verse in the translations included in this book. Medieval Persian poetry is highly formal – one could say without exaggeration that it makes a fetish of its formality – and the fact that it *is* poetry is considered to reside precisely in such formal, technical considerations. The twelfth-century poet Shatranji says in one of his rubaiyat, "The beauty of a verse is in its rhyme," and it would be hard to find a medieval Persian poet who would have had much of a quarrel with this. Shatranji's name means "the chess player"; rhymes, and the complicated, elegant, rule-generated game of chess are together a good image for what a medieval Persian lyric tends to be like. There is a virtuosic element in the formality of even the simplest medieval Persian poems, and if a translator is to convey what such poems are like in the original, he needs to make at least a gesture in this direction.

Metrical poetry in English has many forms (the sonnet, the ballad, the heroic couplet, and so on), but only two meters that are at all common (iambic and its derivative iambic/anapestic, and trochaic); Persian poetry has many meters (Hafez, for example, uses in all twenty-three different meters, though some of them only once), but only two forms – monorhyme and the couplet. All Persian poetic forms are variants of one of these two (a few rare forms include both monorhyme and the couplet). In general, narrative poems are written in couplets, while all other poems are written in some form of monorhyme (that is, the same rhyme sound is used throughout the whole poem).

The great majority of the poems included here are translations of ghazals, which is a monorhymed form. A ghazal is a lyric poem, as we have seen, usually of between seven and twenty lines. Persian poetic lines are very long compared with lines in English verse, and they are divided into two half-lines; usually each of these half-lines is equivalent in length to a complete (and long) English verse line. For example, over seventy percent of Hafez's ghazals are made up of half-lines that contain fourteen or fifteen syllables, and so have twenty-eight or thirty syllables to the complete line. In a ghazal the first two half-lines rhyme, and after this the same rhyme comes at the end of each complete line, but not within the line.

How to give some indication of this form in English, if one wishes to do so, is obviously a problem. I have to get a little technical here, and the reader who is not interested in verse technique is welcome to skip the rest of this paragraph and the next two. First we need to bear in mind that a half-line in a Persian lyric tends to be made up of around fourteen syllables. And it so happens that there is a fourteen-syllable line, called, unsurprisingly, the fourteener, in English prosody; it is, for example, the form into which the sixteenth-century translator George Chapman cast his version of the *Iliad*. The fourteener in its original form is now rare, but it has continued to exist in a "broken" form in the ballad stanza, which is typically made up of two fourteeners, "broken" as 8/6, 8/6. This gives us twenty-eight syllables, the complete line length of a great many lines in Persian ghazals. Although it might look very far from the original form, I have translated many of the lines of the ghazals in this book as ballad stanzas, or as close approximations (sometimes breaking in a different place, for example 10/4, or with a slightly different number of syllables, for example 8/4). Strangely enough, this does, I think, give some notion of the rhythm of the Persian. The half-line itself in Persian often has a natural pause around its middle (corresponding to the caesura in an English verse line), and the equivalent of this is indicated by the break within the fourteener in the translations. This break is less emphatic than the stronger break between the fourteeners – that is, between lines 2 and 3 of the English stanza – corresponding to the break between the two half-lines in Persian. The approximation of rhythm is of course little more than this, mainly because English meter is accentual (based on syllabic stress) and Persian meter is quantitative (based on syllabic length); nevertheless the use of this form does, I feel, usually bring a reader closer to the rhythmic movement of the Persian than any other English form is able to do. Even so, I haven't translated all the ghazals in this way, as other forms sometimes seemed equally or more apposite, particularly for poems written in shorter lines than the more usual twenty-eight or thirty syllables. I have translated a number of poems as simple couplets, with one couplet in English equaling two half-lines in the Persian. Sometimes, when the lines seemed naturally to form themselves into groups, I have arranged the lines as stanzas to indicate this, although the reader should be aware that there are no "stanzas" in the Persian.

What can a translator do about monorhyme? This rhyme scheme is relatively rare in English poetry; indeed there are probably only two well-known monorhymed poems in the canon of English verse, both from the late nineteenth century: Tennyson's beautiful "Frater, Ave Atque Vale" ("Brother, Hail and Farewell"), written as an evocation of Catullus, and Browning's "Home Thoughts from the Sea."[13] Both are about Englishmen abroad (Tennyson in Italy, Browning in a ship off the coast of Spain), as if the poets associated the form with foreign, non-English, experiences. Tennyson's use of monorhyme may possibly owe something to the Persian model; he was for many years a close friend of Edward FitzGerald, the Victorian translator of *The Rubaiyat of Omar Khayyam*, and for a while he tried to learn Persian. (He had dreams of Persian letters parading around his room; unfortunately his wife thought Persian was bad for his eyes, and hid his Persian books, which put a stop to the venture.) These poems by Browning and Tennyson are similar in two other ways. Both use what is by the standards of English verse, a long (fifteen syllable) trochaic line, and this too may be a nod to a Persian model; and both rhyme on vowels unclosed by consonants, which is by far the easiest kind of monorhyme that can be attempted in English. I have tried monorhyme for some of the versions in this book, and

---

13. Monorhyme has, however, flourished in popular music in the last few decades, and again the example of Bob Dylan is relevant. Dylan often uses monorhyme for long stretches of his songs; again Hafez comes to mind in the association of words and music, and also in the way that Dylan's monorhymes can sometimes seem to lead the "plot" of his songs forward, as can also appear to be happening in some Hafez ghazals. More recently, monorhyme is a staple of both rap and hip-hop.

the interested reader will notice that, like Tennyson and Browning, I too have often availed myself of vowel rhymes. Usually, however, I have used a new rhyme for each "stanza" or couplet. Sometimes I have kept the rhyme where it is in Persian (that is, after twenty-eight or thirty syllables), but this is a long stretch to go without a rhyme in English (it can become virtually unnoticeable, which it emphatically isn't in Persian), and usually I have rhymed within the "stanza" or couplet. A number of the translations follow the Persian rhyme scheme exactly – for example, the poem by Jahan Khatun, on p. 179, "I know you think that there are other friends for me than you. Not so."

The rhyme word in this poem is "you," and every time the rhyme appears the phrase, "Not so" comes after it. This device (called a *radif*), of repeating a phrase after each iteration of the rhyme, is quite common in Persian lyric (and epigrammatic) poetry, and I have tried to reproduce it where possible. Its effect is to bury the rhyme within the line, while the repeated phrase is like a richer amplification of the rhyme; the repetitions, coming in such a prominent metrical position, also emphatically underline the meaning of the phrase, which becomes an integral part of the theme of the poem. Sometimes the same phrase can be used with a different meaning in at least one of its repetitions – for example, by a pun on one of its constituent words – and this strategy is particularly prized (it's also particularly hard to translate).

I have remarked above on both the lack of gender markers in Persian, and the androgynous nature of the rhetoric that celebrates human beauty and sexual desirability in Persian poetry. I've drawn attention to the generally pederastic nature of the conventions of this kind of verse, but I have also indicated that when these poets do talk, rarely, about gender directly, what we seem to have is a situation similar to that which we find in some Classical European verse, in which both genders are celebrated with some impartiality. Unfortunately a translator of Persian lyric poetry into English usually has to make a decision as to the gender of the person being addressed in a given poem. Where the gender is, very occasionally, made clear, the decision has been made for me. Otherwise I have been fairly even-handed in my distribution of boys and girls, but the reader should be aware that this is in most cases an arbitrary decision, so that he or she is perfectly welcome to change most instances of "he" to "she" and "she" to "he," as he or she wishes.

Acknowledgments and Further Reading

There is little on either Jahan Malek Khatun or Obayd-e Zakani in English. For information on Jahan Khatun and the milieu in which she lived I have consulted the admirable articles on her life and poetry by Dominic Brookshaw (his article on her in the *Encyclopedia Iranica*, and his "Odes of a Poet-Princess: the Ghazals of Jahan-Malik Khatun," Iran 43, 2005, pp. 173–95). Apart from these, my main source for information on Jahan has been the introduction to her Divan, edited by Dr. Purandokht Kashani-Rad and Dr. Kamel Ahmadnezhad (Tehran: Zavar, 1374 / 1995). Hasan Javadi's book on Obayd-e Zakani, *Obeyd-e Zakani: Ethics of the Aristocrats and Other Satirical Works* (Washington, D.C.: Mage Publishers, 2008) has been an invaluable source of information, not only on Obayd but on the literary life of Shiraz in the fourteenth century. Paul Sprachman has written entertainingly on Obayd, notably in his *Suppressed Persian* (Costa Mesa: Mazda, 1995). A great deal has been written about Hafez, but not much that is useful in English; the best source in English for information on Hafez is the excellent series of essays on his poetry and life in the *Encyclopedia Iranica*. There are valuable discussions of the structure of Hafez's ghazals in Michael C. Hillmann, *Unity in the Ghazals of Hafez*, (Minneapolis: Bibliotheca Islamica, 1976), and Julie Meisami has written a number of illuminating essays on Hafez's verse. I have consulted various commentaries on Hafez's poetry in Persian, including the oldest, by Sudi in the Persian translation of the Turkish text by Dr. Esmat Setarzadeh, *Sharh-e Sudi bar Hafez* (Tehran: Enzali, 1362/1983), as well as a number of contemporary examples of the genre. The French translation of Hafez's Divan, together with an extensive commentary, by Charles–Henri Fouchécour, *Le Divan* (Paris: Éditions Verdier, 2006), is an encyclopedically helpful source, although it can sometimes stress mystical/ Sufi interpretations at the expense of more literal readings. For general information on the city of Shiraz in the 14th century I am indebted to John Limbert's *Shiraz in the Age of Hafez* (Seattle: University of Washington Press, 2004), a book I cannot praise too highly. Many friends have given me help and advice over the years that I have worked on the translations included here. My chief personal debts are indicated in the dedication, but I must also single out for particular mention the many useful and sometimes brilliant suggestions made by two poet friends, Catherine Tufariello and Robert Wells, both of whom have read much of this book at different stages of its development. Remaining infelicities and mistranslations are, needless to say, my own.

SOURCES

For the poems of Hafez, I have used mainly the version edited by Parviz Natel Khanlari, *Divan-e Hafez,* in two volumes (Tehran: Kharazmi, 1362/1983), though I have also made comparisons with other editions, notably that edited by Seyyed Abol-Qasem Anjavi-Shirazi, *Divan-e Hafez* (Tehran: Javidan, 1345/1966). For Jahan Khatun's poems, I have used the edition mentioned above (edited by Purandokht Kashani-Rad and Kamel Ahmadnezhad), which is the only edition of her poems to have appeared so far. For most of the poems of Obayd-e Zakani, I have used the version edited by Mohammad Ja`far Mahjub, *Kolliyat-e Obayd-e Zakani* (New York: Biblioteca Persica, 1999); for the text of Obayd's *Cat and Mouse,* I have used the version edited by Parviz Atabeki, *Kolliyat-e Obayd-e Zakani* (Tehran: Farzan, 1343/1964). The text of two of Obayd's poems translated here (pp. lix and 195) is taken from the edition of Amir Dowlatshah Samarqandi's *Tazkirat al-Sho`ara*, edited by Mohammad Ramezani (Tehran: Khavar, 1338/1959).

Poems

Hafez

My friend, hold back your heart from enemies,
Drink shining wine with handsome friends like these;
With art's initiates undo your collar –
Stay buttoned up with ignoramuses.

هر چند پیر و خسته دل و ناتوان شدم

HOWEVER OLD, INCAPABLE,
  And heart-sick I may be,
The moment I recall your face
   My youth's restored to me;

Thanks be to God that all I sought
   From Him I have received,
That my exertions brought to me
   The fortune I've achieved.

Rejoice, young sapling, in your glory,
   For in your shadow there
I am the nightingale whose songs
   Are heard now everywhere.

To me, at first, the heights and depths
   Of Being were unknown,
But schooled within my longing for you
   How well informed I've grown!

Fate drags me to the wine-shop's door –
   And though I turn and twist,
That's where I always finish up;
   It's useless to resist.

It's not that I am old in months
        And years; if truth be told
The friend I love's untrue to me –
        It's this that makes me old.

Within my heart, the door of meaning
        Opened the day I sought
Our ancient Zoroastrian out
        And entered in his court.

On Glory's highway, and upon
        Good Fortune's throne, I raise
The wine-cup, and receive my friends'
        Warm welcome and their praise!

And from that moment that your glance
        First troubled me, I'm sure
I've been immune to all the troubles
        The last days have in store.

Last night God's kindness brought good news –
        "Hafez, I guarantee
That all your sins will be forgiven;
        Come back, return to Me!"

زلف آشفته و خوی کرده و خندان لب و مست

LAST NIGHT SHE BROUGHT ME WINE, AND SAT BESIDE MY PILLOW;
Her hair hung loose, her dress was torn, her face perspired –
She smiled and sang of love, with mischief in her eyes,
And whispering in my ear, she drunkenly inquired:

"My ancient lover, can it be that you're asleep?
The true initiate, when offered wine at night,
Would be a heretic of love if he refused
To take the draught he's given, and drink it with delight."

And as for you, you hypocrites, don't cavil at
Lovers who drain life to the lees, since we were given
This nature when the world began, and we must drink
The wine that's poured for us, whether from earth or heaven.

So take the laughing wine cup, raise it in your hand,
Caress your lover's curls, and say Hafez has spoken;
How many vows of abstinence the world has seen
So fervently affirmed, and – like Hafez's – broken.

❧

گل بی رخ یار خوش نباشد

A FLOWER, WITHOUT A FRIEND'S FACE THERE, I THINK
> that isn't good

And springtime, if there isn't wine to drink,
> that isn't good

A stroll through gardens, or a wooded place,
Without a pretty tulip-blushing face
> that isn't good

A cypress swaying, and a rose unfolding,
Without a nightingale's melodious scolding
> that isn't good

A sweet-lipped, sexy lover near, if this is
To be with no embraces and no kisses
> that isn't good

Wine in a garden can be sweet, but when
We have no friend to talk and listen, then
> that isn't good

And anything the mind dreams, in the end,
Unless it is the features of our friend,
> that isn't good

The soul's a useless coin, Hafez – not worth
Your casting, as an offering, on the earth
> that isn't good

یاری اندر کس نمی بینم یاران را چه شد

I SEE NO LOVE IN ANYONE,
Where, then, have all the lovers gone?
And when did all our friendship end,
And what's become of every friend?

Life's water's muddied now, and where
Is Khezr to guide us from despair?
The rose has lost its coloring,
What's happened to the breeze of spring?

A hundred thousand flowers appear
But no birds sing for them to hear –
Thousands of nightingales are dumb:
Where are they now? Why don't they come?

For years no rubies have been found
In stony mines deep underground;
When will the sun shine forth again?
Where are the clouds brimful of rain?

Gone are the sweet songs Venus made –
Can she have burned the lute she played?
Who thinks of drinking now? No one.
Where have the roistering drinkers gone?

This was a town of lovers once,
Of kindness and benevolence,
And when did kindness end? What brought
The sweetness of our town to naught?

The ball of generosity
Lies on the field for all to see –
No rider comes to strike it; where
Is everyone who should be there?

Silence Hafez, since no one knows
The secret ways that heaven goes;
Who is it that you're asking how
The heavens are revolving now?

صحن بستان ذوق بخش و صحبت یاران خوش است

THE ORCHARD CHARMS OUR HEARTS, AND CHATTER WHEN
  our dearest friends appear – is sweet;

God bless the time of roses! To drink our wine
  among the roses here – is sweet!

Our souls' scent sweetens with each breeze; ah yes,
  the sighs that lovers hear – are sweet.

Sing, nightingale! Rosebuds unopened yet
  will leave you, and your fear – is sweet;

Dear singer of the night, for those in love
  your sad lament is clear – and sweet.

The world's bazaar contains no joy, except
  the libertine's; good cheer – is sweet!

I heard the lilies say, "The world is old,
  to take things lightly here – is sweet."

Hafez, the happy heart ignores the world;
  don't think dominion here – is sweet.

بُرد از من قرار و طاقت و هوش

SWEET LIPS AND SILVER EARS – THAT IDOL'S ELEGANCE
Has snatched away my fortitude, and my good sense;

So lovely, lithe, and lively, such a fairy face,
That Turk in his cute cloak, all wiles and nonchalance –

And I'm so mad about him, so on fire for him,
I'm like a cooking cauldron's seething turbulence,

But I'll calm down when I can grab that cloak from him
And be the shirt that covers up his impudence.

And when my bones are rotting, still my soul will not
Forget his kindness to me, his benevolence.

His chest and shoulders, chest and shoulders, bore away
My faith and heart, my faith and heart – I'd no defense!

So here's your medicine, Hafez, here's your medicine now –
Sweet lips, sweet lips, sweet lips are your deliverance!

الا يا أيها الساقي ادر كأساً وناولها

COME, BOY, AND PASS THE WINE AROUND —
   Love seemed a simple game
When I encountered it . . . but then
   The difficulties came!

In longing for the musky scent
   The breeze brings from her hair,
Such blood wells up in lovers' hearts,
   Such suffering, and despair . . .

What can ensure my happiness,
   At love's stage, in my heart?
When every instant now the bell
   Cries, "Load up, to depart!"

And if the wine-seller says wine
   Should dye your prayer-mat . . . dye it!
Pilgrims should know each stage's rule
   And seek to satisfy it.

On this dark night, amidst these waves,
   The whirlpool's fearsome roar,
What can they know of our distress
   Who watch us from the shore?

In all I've done, I've pleased myself,
   It's ruined my good name –
The secret's out, and everywhere
   Men talk about my shame.

Don't hide from Him you seek, Hafez;
   You cannot hope to find
The One you're longing for until
   You leave the world behind.

❧

روی تو کس ندید و هزارت رقیب هست

NO ONE HAS SEEN YOUR FACE, AND YET
   Thousands of rivals seek you;
You're still a bud and yet a hundred
   Nightingales entreat you.

However far I am from you
   (May no one know that place!)
I cannot help but hope that soon
   I'll be in your embrace;

And it's not strange that I should choose
   Your street in which to wait –
Thousands of strangers in this world
   Are in the selfsame state.

The loved one doesn't spare a glance –
   The lover must endure it;
And there's no pain, or if there is
   The doctor's here to cure it.

In love, the Sufi meeting house
   And wine-shop are one place;
As are all places where we find
   The loved one's radiant face;

And what the Sufis make a show of
    Can be found equally
Among the monks, before their cross,
    Within a monastery.

Hafez's cry is not mere nonsense
    When all is said and done;
Though it's a strangely curious tale,
    And a perplexing one.

TO TELL YOU NOW MY POOR HEART'S STATE
> is what I long for

To hear the news that hearts relate
> is what I long for

Look how naïve I am! To keep from rivals' ears
A tale the winds disseminate
> is what I long for

To sleep a sweet and noble night with you, to sleep
Till morning and to rise up late
> is what I long for

And in the darkness of the night, to pierce the pearl
That is so fine and delicate
> is what I long for

O morning breeze, abet me now, tonight, because
To blossom as dawn lies in wait
> is what I long for

To use the lashes of my eyes, for honor's sake,
To sweep the dust before your gate
> is what I long for

Like Hafez, in contempt of prigs, to make the kind
Of poem libertines create
> is what I long for

THANKS BE TO GOD NOW THAT THE WINE-SHOP DOOR
Is open, since it's there I'm heading for;

The jars are groaning with fermented wine,
With wine that's real, and not a metaphor,

That brings us drunkenness, and pride, and pleasure,
While we bring weakness, need, and not much more!

The secret I've not told, and won't, to others
I'll tell my friend – of him I can be sure.

It's not a short tale, it describes the twists
In my belovèd's hair, and lovers' lore,

Majnun's grief, Layla's curls, Ayaz's foot
That royal Mahmud's face bowed down before;

And like a hawk I've seeled my eyes to all
The world, to glimpse the face that I adore.

Whoever strays within your street, it is
Your eyebrow's curve that he will pray before;

O friends, to know the fire in Hafez' heart
Ask candles what they're burning, melting, for.

گل در بر و می در کف و معشوق به کام است

WINE IN MY GLASS, AND ROSES IN MY ARMS,
        my lover near me –
On such a day the world's great king would be
        my slave and fear me.

No need to bring a candle to
        our meeting place tonight;
My friend is there, the full moon of his face
        will be our light.

Though wine in our religion's not forbidden
        (never think it!),
If you're not there, my cypress-slender love,
        how can I drink it?

Don't sprinkle perfume where we meet –
        the tresses of your hair
Each moment spread the fragrance of
        such sweetness there . . .

My ears hear only plaintive flute-notes
        and the harp's sweet sound;
My eyes see only ruby lips
        and wine-cups going round.

Don't talk to me of sugar, or
                    of any food that's sweet;
Sweetness for me is on your lips
                    when your and my lips meet.

I'll haunt these ruins while within
                    the ruins of my heart
The treasure of my love for you
                    is lodged and won't depart.

Why do you talk to me of shame — shame
                    has become my name —
Or reputation, when my reputation
                    is my shame?

We drink our wine, we flirt, and we're
                    licentious — yes, but who
Is in this city where we live
                    of whom this isn't true?

And don't go to the morals officer
                    to make a fuss —
He's on the constant lookout too for pleasure,
                    just like us.

This is no time to sit, Hafez,
                    without your wine and lover;
Jasmine's and roses' days are here,
                    and Ramadan is over.

برو به کار خود ای واعظ این چه فریادست

GO, MIND YOUR OWN BUSINESS, PREACHER! WHAT'S ALL
   This hullabaloo?
My heart has left the road you travel, but
   What's that to you?

Until my lips are played on like a flute
   By his lips' beauty,
My ears can only hear as wind the world's
   Advice on duty –

God made him out of nothing, and within
   His being's state
There is a mystery no being's skill
   Can penetrate.

The beggar in your street disdains eight heavens
   For what he's given;
The captive in your chains is free of this world
   And of heaven;

And even though the drunkenness of love
   Has ruined me,
My being's built upon those ruins for
   Eternity.

My heart, don't whine so often that your friend's
    Unjust to you;
This is the fate he's given you, and this
    Is justice too.

Be off with you, Hafez! Enough of all
    These tales you tell;
I've heard these tales and fables many times;
    I know them well.

خوش آمد گل و زان خوشتر نباشد

WELCOME, SWEET FLOWER, NO ONE'S
  More welcome in this land –
The more so since you hold
  A wine-cup in your hand.

Enjoy this moment's happiness,
  Savor it well;
The pearl will not remain
  Forever in its shell.

Grasp your good fortune! Drink
  Among the flowers, since they
Will all have fled before
  A week has passed away.

If you can fill a golden bowl
  With wine now, give
Its draught to one who lacks
  The gold with which to live.

Come, sheikh, and join in our
  Carousing – you'll be given
A draught of wine that you
  Won't ever find in heaven;

To learn with us, wipe clean
    Your schoolbook's pages; look –
The knowledge lovers learn
    Is not in any book.

Hear what I say now, tie
    Your heart to some sweet boy
Whose beauty's not applied,
    Whose prettiness won't cloy.

O God, I pray, give me
    A wine that will not make
Me drunk and crapulous,
    Or cause my head to ache.

The man who'd criticize
    Hafez's poetry
Must have a brutal soul
    Devoid of charity!

My soul's a slave in thrall
    To my Sultan Ovays,
And if he has forgotten me
    That's still the case,

And by his crown I swear
    The sun itself can't claim
A diadem more bright
    And glorious than his name.

❧

بیا تا گل برافشانیم و می در ساغر اندازیم

COME, SO THAT WE CAN SCATTER FLOWERS
    and fill the glass with wine,
And split the ceiling of the skies
    and try a new design!

If Sorrow sends her soldiers here
    and wants a bloody fight,
My serving boy and I will put
    them one and all to flight.

We'll add rose water to our wine
    and sugar will augment
The pungent aloes wood we burn,
    and sweeten its fierce scent.

A fine lute's in your hand, my friend,
    so give us a fine song –
We'll wave our hands and stamp our feet,
    and dance, and sing along!

Sweet breeze, convey the dust of our
    existence to that place
Where Splendor reigns – perhaps that way
    we'll see Him face to face . . .

One boasts about his intellect,
      one's all puffed up with pride;
Let's bring these arguments before
      our Judge – let Him decide.

Come join me in the wine-shop, friend,
      if you want paradise;
I'll tip you from the wine-cask to
      Kosar's stream in a trice.

Since in Shiraz poetic skill,
      Hafez, goes unrequited,
It's time to try another town
      whose court is less benighted.

❧

منم که گوشهٔ میخانه خانقاه من است

A CORNER OF THE WINE-SHOP IS
  the temple where I pray;
My morning plea's the prayer
  the Zoroastrians say;

And if I miss the harp at dawn
  I needn't worry now –
My waking song's my prayerful sigh
  and my repentant vow.

Thank God I care for neither king
  nor beggar! since I see
The poorest beggar at my friend's
  door is a king to me.

All I require from mosque and wine-shop
  is to know your love;
As God's my witness, this is all
  that I've been dreaming of –

And since I've bowed my head down to
  this threshold, I have known
The heavenly sun itself is where
  I'm seated on my throne.

Until death's dagger rends the tent
   that is my life, my heart
Will not abjure his doorway – no,
   I cannot now depart.

Though sin's not ours to choose, Hafez,
   keep to the disciplined
And noble way you've traveled on,
   and say, "It's I who've sinned."

بغیر از آنکه بشد دین و دانش از دستم

COME, TELL ME WHAT IT IS THAT I HAVE GAINED
  From loving you,
Apart from losing all the faith I had
  And knowledge too?

Though longing for you scatters on the wind
  All my life's work,
Still, by the dust on your dear feet, I have
  Kept faith with you.

And even though I'm just a tiny mote
  In love's great kingdom,
I'm one now with the sun, before your face,
  In loving you.

Bring wine! In all my life I've never known
  A corner where
I could sit snugly, safely, and enjoy
  Contentment too.

And, if you're sensible, don't ply me with
  Advice; your words
Are wasted on me, and the reason is
  I'm drunk; it's true!

How can I not feel hopeless shame when I
   Am near my love?
What service could I offer him? What could
   I say or do?

Hafez is burned, but his bewitching love
   Has yet to say,
"Hafez, I wounded you, and here's the balm
   I send for you."

روز وصل دوستداران یاد باد

THOSE DAYS WHEN LOVING FRIENDS WOULD MEET —
                    long may they be recalled!
Those days gone by that were so sweet —
                    long may they be recalled!

My palate's bitter with grief's aftertaste: those cries
With which we drinkers would compete —
                    long may they be recalled!

And even though my friends have all forgotten me,
A thousand times I will repeat,
                    "Long may they be recalled!"

I'm wretched now, quite overthrown; the struggles of
My noble friends, in my defeat —
                    long may they be recalled!

My eyes run with a hundred streams; but Zendehrud,
And Karan's pastoral retreat,
                    long may they be recalled!

Henceforth, Hafez's secrets will remain unspoken,
Those confidants . . . Oh, I repeat,
                    "Long may they be recalled!"

یوسف گم‌گشته بازآید به کنعان غم مخور

LOST JOSEPH WILL RETURN TO CANAAN'S LAND AGAIN
    – do not despair
His grieving father's house will fill with flowers again
    – do not despair

O sorrow-stricken heart, your fortunes will revive,
Order will come to your distracted mind again
    – do not despair

And if the heavens turn against us for two days
They turn, and will not stay forever in one place
    – do not despair

Sweet singing bird, survive until the spring, and then
You'll tread on grass again, deep in the flowers' shade
    – do not despair

Don't give up hope, you have no knowledge of Fate's lore;
Behind the veil who knows what hidden turns still wait?
    – do not despair

When, if you long to tread the pilgrims' desert trail
To Mecca's distant shrine, sharp thorns beset your path
    – do not despair

For God, who solves all sorrows, knows the sorrows of
Our absence and desire, the guardian's scornful rage
  – do not despair

O heart, if nothingness should wash away the world,
Since Noah guides your craft, when you encounter storms
  – do not despair

And though the journey's filled with dangers, and its goal
Is all unknown, there is no road that has no end
  – do not despair

O Hafez, in night's darkness, alone, in poverty,
While the Qur'an remains to you, and murmured prayer
  – do not despair

دوش آگهی ز یار سفر کرده داد باد

LAST NIGHT, NEWS OF MY DEPARTED FRIEND
Was brought to me upon the wind;
Whatever must come, let it come!
I give my heart now to the wind.

My life's in such a state that my
Companions are the vivid flash
Of lightning in the dark of night,
And, as each dawn arrives, the wind.

Lost in the tangles of your hair
My shameless heart has never said,
"Oh, give me back the life I knew
Before I strayed like this, and sinned."

My heart weeps blood remembering you,
Each time I see the meadows where
The budding rose's cloak is loosed
And torn wide open by the wind.

My frail existence vanishes;
But may my soul rejoice again
And see you, and inhale your scent
Brought in the dawn, upon the wind.

Hafez, your noble nature will
Ensure your heart's desire; and may
Our lives be given to such sweetness,
That's borne away, upon the wind.

Hafez • 31

WHAT'S ALL THIS HIDING HAPPINESS AND WINE AWAY?
I've lined up with the libertines now, come what may.

Undo your heart's knot, and ignore the heavens: since no
Astronomer's undone *that* knot yet, let it go!

Don't wonder at the revolutions we've lived through;
Time's fashioned thousands of such fables – they're not new!

But take the wine-cup reverently, since in your hand
Is Jamshid's skull, and King Qobad's, who ruled this land.

Who knows where Kay Kavus, or Bahman, have now gone?
Or what wind swept away King Jamshid's royal throne?

From Farhad's blood-red tears I see the tulips bloom –
He longs still for Shirin's sweet lips, within his tomb.

You'd say the tulips know time's treachery – since all
Their life they're like a wine-glass, till their petals fall.

Come quickly, come, this wine will ruin us one day,
Unless these ruins hold a treasure – who can say?

Mosalla's breeze, and Roknabad's clear stream, have told me
I cannot leave this town; they will forever hold me.

Like Hafez, don't drink till you hear the harp's sweet sound
To which, with silken threads, his happy heart is bound.

درد عشقی کشیده‌ام که مپرس

I'VE KNOWN THE PAINS OF LOVE'S FRUSTRATION – AH, DON'T ASK!
I've drained the dregs of separation – ah, don't ask!

I've been about the world and found at last
A lover worthy of my adoration – ah, don't ask!

So that my tears now lay the dust before
Her door in constant supplication – ah, don't ask!

Last night, with my own ears, I heard such words
Fall from her in our conversation – ah, don't ask!

You bite your lip at me? The lip I bite
Is all delicious delectation! – ah, don't ask!

Without you, in this beggarly poor hut,
I have endured such desolation – ah, don't ask!

Lost on love's road, like Hafez, I've attained
A stage . . . but stop this speculation – ah, don't ask!

❧

عیب رندان مکن ای زاهد پاکیزه سرشت

THAT YOU'RE A PIOUS PRIG BY NATURE
    Doesn't mean you have to blame
Libertines for their faults; those sins
    Won't be imputed to your name.

Each one of us will reap the seeds
    He sows, so what is it to you
Whether I'm good or bad? To work on who
    You are should be your aim.

Everyone searches for the Friend,
    Whether they're drunk or stone-cold sober;
And love's in every house – the mosque
    And synagogue are just the same.

I bow my head in worship on the bricks
    That form the wine-shop's threshold;
And if that blockhead doesn't get it, then
    It's him who is to blame!

Don't sadden me with tales of providence
    And God's eternal promise –
What do you know of who, behind the veil,
    Can boast of beauty's name?

It's not just me who's wandered out
       Of lonely Piety's front door;
My father let his chance of heaven's grace
       Elude him; I'm the same.

If this is who you are, the nature
       You were given, then bravo!
And good for you if your fine character's
       Exactly as you claim!

O Hafez, on the last day, if you bear
       A wine-cup in your hand,
You'll go straight into heaven from the street
       Of drunkenness and shame.

مزرع سبز فلک دیدم و داس مه نو

I SAW THE GREEN FIELDS OF THE SKY,
     and there a sickle moon –
I reckoned what I'd sown, and thought,
     "The harvest will come soon."

I said, "My luck, you've been asleep;
     now dawn has brought the sun."
She said, "The past is past; do not
     despair of all you've done;

The night you leave this world, go, climb
     like Jesus through the skies –
Your lamp, a hundred times, will light
     the sun as you arise.

Don't trust the shining moon, she is
     the highway robber who
Stole Kay Kavus's throne, and then
     the belt of Khosrow too.

Gold earrings set with rubies may
     charm you, and lead you on,
But know this: Beauty's reign is brief,
     and all too quickly gone."

God keep the evil eye from your
        sweet beauty, which can field
A pawn to make the sun and moon
        precipitously yield.

Say to the heavens, "Don't boast of splendor!"
        When love is matched with you,
The harvest of the moon's a grain,
        and of the stars but two.

Hypocrisy will burn the harvest
        religion reaped; and so,
Hafez, shrug off this Sufi cloak –
        just leave now, let it go.

خوشتر ز عیش و صحبت و باغ و بهار چیست

WHAT'S SWEETER THAN A GARDEN AND GOOD TALK
When spring's new flowers appear?
What's keeping that young boy who serves our wine?
Tell me why he's not here.

Put down as profit every happy moment
That Fate contrives to send;
Who has a notion what awaits us when
Our lives here have to end?

And understand, life hangs here by a hair;
That what you have to do
Is take care of yourself; since what are Time
And all its griefs to you?

The Water of Life, the Garden of Eram –
What could these blessings mean
But heart-delighting wine that's poured and drunk
Beside some pretty stream?

Since abstinence and drunkenness share one
Descent, which has our voice?
Which should we give our skittish hearts to now?
What could decide our choice?

Who knows what lies beyond the veil? And your
          Long boastful rant before
Its chamberlain, what point has that, you fool?
          Shut up! Not one word more!

And if I've sinned and strayed, and there's
          A reckoning when I die,
What is it the Creator's clemency
          And mercy signify?

The ascetic longs to drink from Kosar's stream
          In paradise's shade,
And Hafez longs for wine; until, between
          The two, God's choice is made.

※

دوش دیدم که ملایک در میخانه زدند

LAST NIGHT I SAW THE ANGELS
   tapping at the wine-shop's door,
And kneading Adam's dust,
   and molding it as cups for wine;

And, where I sat beside the road,
   these messengers of heaven
Gave me their wine to drink,
   so that their drunkenness was mine.

The heavens could not bear
   the heavy trust they had been given,
And lots were cast, and crazed
   Hafez's name received the sign.

Forgive the seventy-two
   competing factions – all their tales
Mean that the Truth is what
   they haven't seen, and can't define!

But I am thankful that there's peace
   between Him now, and me;
In celebration of our pact
   the houris drink their wine –

And fire is not what gently smiles
    from candles' flames, it's what
Annihilates the flocking moths
    that flutter round His shrine.

No one has drawn aside the veil
    of Thought as Hafez has,
Or combed the curls of Speech
    as his sharp pen has, line by line.

ساليها دل طلب جام جم از مای كرد

FOR YEARS MY HEART INQUIRED OF ME
Where Jamshid's sacred cup might be,
And what was in its own possession
It asked from strangers, constantly;
Begging the pearl that's slipped its shell
From lost souls wandering by the sea.

Last night I took my troubles to
The Magian sage whose keen eyes see
A hundred answers in the wine;
Laughing, he showed the cup to me –
I asked him, "When was this cup
That shows the world's reality

Handed to you?" He said, "The day
Heaven's vault of lapis lazuli
Was raised, and marvelous things took place
By Intellect's divine decree,
And Moses' miracles were made
And Sameri's apostasy."

He added then, "That friend they hanged
High on the looming gallows tree –
His sin was that he spoke of things
Which should be pondered secretly;
The page of truth his heart enclosed
Was annotated publicly.
But if the Holy Ghost once more

Should lend his aid to us, we'd see
Others perform what Jesus did –
    Since in his heart-sick anguish he
Was unaware that God was there
    And called His name out ceaselessly."

I asked him next, "And beauties' curls
    That tumble down so sinuously,
What do they mean? Whence do they come?"
    "Hafez," the sage replied to me,
"Their source is your distracted heart
    That asks these questions constantly."

❧

دوش وقت سحر از غصّه نجاتم دادند

LAST NIGHT, AT DAWN, IN MY DISTRESS, SALVATION
$\qquad$ was given to me;
In darkness then, life's water, a libation,
$\qquad$ was given to me.

Rapt from myself by that pure lambent light,
The wine of essence, and of all creation,
$\qquad$ was given to me.

O dawn of Fortune, moment of pure Glory,
That night when notice of my liberation
$\qquad$ was given to me!

I gazed in Beauty's mirror then, for there
My essence, shining for my contemplation,
$\qquad$ was given to me.

If I was happy then, it's no surprise –
I was deserving, and a just donation
$\qquad$ was given to me.

That day a heavenly voice brought me good news;
The strength to bear this harsh world's subjugation
$\qquad$ was given to me.

It was Hafez's spirit, and the sighs of those
Who rise at dawn, by which, at last, salvation
$\qquad$ was given to me.

یارم چو قدح به دست گیرد

WHEN MY LOVE LIFTS HIS GLASS,
 throughout the town
Love's market suddenly
 comes tumbling down.

I wept before his feet;
 I could not stand –
Would he so much as lend
 a helping hand?

I was a fish, I fell
 into the sea
So that my lover's hook
 would lodge in me;

And anyone who saw
 his eyes would say;
"Where's the police, to haul
 this drunk away?"

Happy the heart that lifts
 a glass of wine
Whose vintage, like Hafez's,
 is divine.

PLANT FRIENDSHIP'S TREE – THE HEART'S DESIRE
  Is the fruit it bears;

And uproot enmity – which brings
  Sorrows and cares.

Be friendly, easy, with drunkards –
  Good fellowship's theirs;

It's pride brings the hangover, not
  The wine-seller's wares.

Talk with your friends, deep in the night,
  And see how life fares;

Since when we are gone the heavens
  Will bring others our cares;

And welcome the spring in your heart
  Since the world never spares

To provide for us roses and songbirds,
  Whoever despairs.

O God, persuade the guide who guards
  The palanquin that bears

Layli within its depths to lead her to
  Majnun – answer his prayers!

Your heart is so tired! You feel caught
   In the weary world's snares

But sip at your wine, and hear in your heart
   The hope it declares:

That Hafez will sit in his orchard
   By the stream that he shares

With his cypress-slim love, God willing,
   In the place that is theirs.

من ترک عشق و شاهد و ساغر نمی کنم

TO GIVE UP WINE, AND HUMAN BEAUTY? AND TO GIVE UP LOVE?
No, I won't do it.
A hundred times I said I would; what was I thinking of?
No, I won't do it.

To say that paradise, its houris, and its shade are more
To me than is the dusty street before my lover's door?
No, I won't do it.

Sermons, and wise men's words, are signs, and that's
how we should treat them;
I mouthed such metaphors before, but now – I won't
repeat them;
No, I won't do it.

I'll never understand myself, I'll never really know me,
Until I've joined the wine-shop's clientele, and that will
show me;
I have to do it.

The preacher told me, "Give up wine" – contempt was
in the saying;
"Sure," I replied. Why should I listen to these
donkeys braying?
No, I won't do it.

The sheikh was angry when he told me, "Give up
   love!" My brother,
There's no end to our arguing about it, so why bother?
               And I won't do it.

My abstinence is this: that when I wink and smile at
   beauty
It won't be from the pulpit in the mosque – I know
   my duty;
               No, I won't do it.

Hafez, good fortune's with the Magian sage, and I
   am sure
I'll never cease to kiss the dust that lies before his door;
               No, I won't do it.

مرا به رندی و عشق آن فضول عیب کند

THAT BUSYBODY CRITICIZES ME
  For loving love and revelry –
But it's my knowledge of the hidden world
  That motivates his enmity:

Don't only look at faults and weaknesses,
  See love in its totality –
It's the untalented who always notice
  Transgressions and deformity.

The fragrance of a houri's borne upon
  The wind now, and caresses me;
She dabs our tavern's dirt inside her collar
  Because its scent is heavenly –

And when our serving boy's all smiles and winks
  He slaps Islam's austerity
So hard that even Sohayb wouldn't shun
  The red wine that he serves to me!

When friends meet heart to heart, this is the key
  To happiness's treasury;
May no one hesitate at such a time
  Or hold back then, reluctantly.

The stories Hafez tells provoke our tears,
    That fall, blood-red, since he
Recalls the time that lies between our youth
    And our white-haired senility.

نوش کن جام شراب یک منی

DRINK WINE DOWN BY THE GLASSFUL, AND YOU'LL TEAR

Out of your heart the roots of your despair –

Keep your heart open, like your glass, not sealed up

Like a flagon, stoppered and doctrinaire;

Drink down the wine of self-forgetfulness;

You'll boast less once you're not so self-aware.

Be stone-like in your steps, not like a cloud

That shifts its colors, gadding everywhere;

But give your heart to wine, and like a man

Sever the necks of frauds obsessed with prayer

Rise, struggle like Hafez . . . And when you find

Your love, prostrate yourself before her there.

عشق تو نهال حیرت آمد

MY LOVE FOR YOU IS LIKE A YOUTHFUL TREE
                              of wonder
And meeting you is all that there can be
                              of wonder

My consciousness is now so drowned within
Our meeting that it's like a whelming sea
                              of wonder

Neither the meeting nor the one who meets
Remain within this spectral fantasy
                              of wonder

Show me one face that seeks for him, that lacks
The dark mole of our incredulity
                              and wonder

And everywhere, from every side, I've heard
These searching questions put perpetually
                              in wonder

From head to toe Hafez's being lives
Within his love for this same youthful tree
                              of wonder

❧

صبا وقت سحر بوئی ز زلف یار می آورد

AT DAWN, UPON THE BREEZE, I CAUGHT
    the scent of my belovèd's hair,
And once again my crazy heart
    was laboring in its old despair.

Out of the garden of my breast
    I've torn his sapling silhouette,
Since when my longings for him blossom,
    grief is the bitter fruit they set.

Fearing the torment of his love,
    I freed my heart from him; but when
My heart dripped blood, the path its drops
    marked out . . . led back to him again.

I saw the full moon rise above
    his castle's roof, splendid and bright;
But when his shining sun arose,
    the moon, for shame, concealed its light.

I took musicians at their word,
    and always, everywhere, I sought
For messengers who'd traveled love's
    hard road, and all the news they brought.

My lover's way, from end to end,
        is good and kind, and little cares
Whether a man tells Moslem beads
        or murmurs Christian prayers.

I was amazed to see Hafez
        drink wine last night; but then I knew
Better than to object to this –
        he drank as secret Sufis do.

May God forgive his eyebrow's curve
        That's made me weak and powerless,
Since it can comfort, with a glance,
        A sick man's feverish distress.

دانی که چنگ و عود چه تقریر می‌کنند

DO YOU KNOW WHAT OUR HARPS AND LUTES ADVISE US,
                    when heard aright?
"Men say that wine's unlawful – when you drink,
                    keep out of sight!"

They say you shouldn't talk of love, or hear
                    love spoken of –
That's a hard lesson that they're teaching us,
                    to give up love.

Love's beauty they despise – and as for lovers,
                    they deride them;
They mock the old, and tell the young that love
                    must be denied them.

I waited at the door, and was deceived
                    a hundred ways,
Longing to know what was decided there,
                    veiled from my gaze.

They pester the old Magian priest; look how
                    these devotees
Harass the old man with their scorn, and their
                    impieties . . .

One glance can buy a hundred different forms
                              of honor's name —
And in this business it's the pretty girls
                              who are to blame.

Some strive and strain and struggle to be with
                              the longed-for friend,
And others are content to let Fate send
                              what it will send.

But when all's said and done, don't trust the world's
                              fidelity,
Since it's a workshop where all things are changed
                              perpetually.

Bring wine! Qur'an reciters, clerics, sheikhs,
                              religion's spies —
Look well at each of them, and see a man
                              who lives by lies.

یاد باد آنکه سرکوی توام منزل بود

WHAT MEMORIES! I ONCE LIVED ON
　　　the street that you lived on,
And to my eyes how bright the dust
　　　before your doorway shone!

We were a lily and a rose:
　　　our talk was then so pure
That what was hidden in your heart
　　　and what I said were one!

And when our hearts discoursed
　　　with Wisdom's ancient words,
Love's commentary solved each crux
　　　within our lexicon.

I told my heart that I would never be
　　　without my friend;
But when our efforts fail, and hearts
　　　Are weak, what can be done?

Last night, for old times' sake, I saw
　　　the place where we once drank;
A cask was lying there, its lees
　　　like blood; mud was its bung.

How much I wandered, asking why
      the pain of parting came –
But Reason was a useless judge,
      and answers? He had none.

And though it's true the turquoise seal
      of Bu Es'haq shone brightly,
His splendid kingdom and his reign
      were all too quickly gone.

Hafez, you've seen a strutting partridge
      whose cry sounds like a laugh –
He's careless of the hawk's sharp claws
      by which he'll be undone.

اگرچه باده فرح بخش و باد گلبیزست

THOUGH WINE IS PLEASURABLE, AND THOUGH THE BREEZE
  Seems soaked in roses, see your harp
Is silent when you drink – because the ears
  Of morals officers are sharp!

If you can find a wine jug and a friend,
  Drink sensibly, and with discretion,
Because the dreadful days we're living through
  Are rife with mischief, and oppression.

See that you hide your wine-cup in your sleeve;
  Your jug's lip sheds its wine, blood-red –
And, in the same way, these cruel times ensure
  Red blood is copiously shed.

We'd better wash away the wine stains from
  Our cloaks with tears of penitence –
Now is the season for sobriety,
  For days of pious abstinence.

The heavens have become a sieve that strains
  Upon us blood, and it is full
Of bloody scraps like royal Khosrow's crown,
  Together with King Kasra's skull.

Don't think that as the heavens turn they'll bring
    A trace of solace or relief;
Their hurtful curvature is through and through
    Made up of wretchedness and grief.

Pars knows the splendor of your verse, Hafez —
    It's made the towns of Eraq glad;
So now's the time to try it out elsewhere —
    Tabriz, perhaps, and then Baghdad.

تنت به ناز طبیبان نیازمند مباد

MAY YOUR DEAR BODY NEVER NEED
        A doctor's expertise,
Your delicate existence know
        No hurtful injuries.

Since all of our horizons' health
        Depends upon your own,
May ill-health never visit you
        With noxious maladies;

And when the wind of autumn blows
        Across these meadows, may
Its passage pass your stature by,
        That's like a cypress tree's;

When your young beauty shows itself,
        May spiteful gossip find
No sneaking opportunity
        To spread its calumnies.

Outward and inward beauty spring
        From your perfections! May
Your form be faultless, and your soul
        Stay free from miseries –

And may the eye of one who casts
                The evil eye on you
Be rue within your beauty's flames,
                Consumed by what it sees.

Your balm is Hafez's sweet words –
                And if you look for these
You won't need rose water again
                Or candied remedies.

گداخت جان که شود کار دل تمام و نشد

TO HAVE MY HEART ACHIEVE ITS GOAL
      grief melted my sad soul – to no effect;
And I was burned within the fire
      of this inane desire – to no effect;

Alas, that in my questing for
      wealth's book, I'm now dirt-poor!
That universal ridicule
      proclaims me sorrow's fool – to no effect!

What pains I suffered as I sought
      admission to his court,
Begging for alms, for charity
      from those who'd comfort me – to no effect;

One night he joked and said, "It's plain
      I'll be your chamberlain!"
Ah, how I've striven to deserve him,
      to be his slave and serve him – to no effect.

He sent word saying that he'd be
      with libertines like me
(Who's called the Dregs-Drinker), so I
      hoped that I'd catch his eye – to no effect.

I dreamed that in my drunkenness
        I might achieve success
And kiss his ruby lips; but all
        I drank was grief and gall – to no effect.

Without good reason never stray
        upon the lovers' way;
How cautiously I've traveled there,
        beset with grief and care – to no effect.

Hafez has tried a thousand wiles,
        a thousand tricks and trials,
Hoping that by his wits and zeal
        He'd bring that boy to heel – to no effect.

حسب حالی نوشتی و شد ایامی چند

YOU'VE SENT NO WORD OF HOW YOU ARE
  It's been a few days . . . quite a few –
And where's our secret go-between
  To take my messages to you?

I know that I can never reach
  To your exalted sanctuary,
Unless your kindness makes you take
  A few steps on the path to me.

The wine is poured into the jug,
  The rose has flung away her veil –
So come now, drink a glass or two,
  Seize joy, let happiness prevail!

Sugar dissolved in rose water
  Won't cure my heart; but if you could
Dissolve your curses in your kisses,
  That distillation surely would.

Ah, puritan, pass by the street
  Of shame, don't let us interrupt you –
Don't linger here with libertines,
  Our sordid chatter might corrupt you!

You've numbered all the faults of wine,
  So number all its virtues too;
Don't throw out wisdom for the sake
  Of what a few drunk oafs might do.

Beggars who crowd the wine-shop door,
  God is your friend; but I advise you,
Don't hope for gifts from cattle who
  Think they're your betters and despise you:

The ancient wine-seller was right
  When he declared, "Don't talk about
The secrets of your smoldering heart
  To every passing, boorish lout."

Hafez's heart is smoldering with
  His passion for your sun-like face;
All Glory's yours, so spare a glance
  For those defeated by disgrace.

نقد صوفی نه همه صافی بی غش باشد

NOT EVERY SUFI'S TRUSTWORTHY, OR PURE IN SPIRIT,
And burning is no more than many of them merit.

Our Sufi prays at dawn, transported with delight,
But watch how drunkenly he welcomes in the night!

Would that a touchstone could display hypocrisy,
Blackening the liar's face with shame, for all to see.

The pampered are not fit to travel on love's road,
Only an outcast's heart can bear the lover's load.

Why let the world upset you? Why, and for how long?
Drink wine, since sorrow in a wise man's heart is wrong.

Our serving boy's young face is ready for its beard –
What tearful faces there will be, once it's appeared!

And if that boy should serve me now, it is a sign
Hafez's cloak and prayer-mat have been sold for wine.

مژده ای دل که مسیحانفسی می آید

GOOD NEWS, MY HEART! THE BREATH OF CHRIST IS WAFTING HERE;
Its sweetness brings the scent of One who'll soon appear.

Don't cry and pray for exile's sake; last night I cast
Our fortune, and an answer to your prayers draws near;

Not only I rejoice within this valley's fire –
Moses, in hopes of borrowed embers, wanders here.

There is no one who has no business in Your street
And all are drawn here by the hopes that they hold dear –

No man can know where his Belovèd now resides,
But still the bell that summons him rings loud and clear;

And if a friend should ask how one grief-stricken fares,
Say, "Well! He's breathing still – he's not yet on his bier."

But ask this garden's nightingale for news, since cries
Of longing from within a cage are all I hear.

My friends, the Friend is hurting Hafez's poor heart;
A falcon hunts a fly, or so it would appear!

دیرست که دلدار پیامی نفرستاد

MY LOVE HAS SENT NO LETTER FOR
   A long time now – I've heard
No salutations from him, no
    Inquiries, not one word;

I've written him a hundred times,
    But that hard-riding king
Has sent no emissary back,
    No message, not a thing!

I'm wild with waiting, crazy, but
    He's sent no envoy here –
No strutting partridge has turned up,
    No graceful, skittish deer.

He knows my heart must now be like
    A fluttering bird, but he
Has yet to send one sinuous line
    To lure and capture me.

Damn him, that sweet-lipped serving boy
    Knows very well that I
Need wine now, but he pours me none,
    Although my glass is dry.

How much I boasted of his favors,
   The kindnesses we'd share –
And now I've no idea at all
   Of how he is, or where.

But this is no surprise, Hafez;
   Calm yourself, and behave!
A king can't be expected to
   Write letters to a slave.

شراب بی غش و ساقّی خوش دو دام رهند

GOOD WINE, THAT DOESN'T STUPEFY,
    That's served by someone pretty – who
Among the wise men of this world
    Escapes the snares set by these two?

It's true, I'm dissolute, in love,
    Known as a shiftless miscreant . . .
A thousand thanks, then, that this town
    Provides friends who are innocent.

If you should step inside our wine-shop,
    Look to your manners while you're there –
The crowd that hangs around its door
    Are the king's cronies, so take care!

Cruelty is not the way of pilgrims,
    Poor men who seek their journey's end;
Bring wine! These "pilgrims" here are going
    Nowhere, for all that they pretend.

But don't despise the beggars lost
    In hopeless love, don't put them down –
They're kings, though this one has no scepter,
    Monarchs, though that one has no crown.

Don't mar your loveliness, don't let
    The glory of your charm be shattered –
You'll find your servants and your slaves
    And all your retinue have scattered.

I am the slave of those who drink
    Life to the dregs, but not of those
Who hide a blackened heart beneath
    The showy splendor of their clothes.

Be ready, for a winnowing wind
    Will blow – none of us shall remain,
And all devotion's thousand harvests
    Will not be worth a barley-grain.

Love is the nobler task – up then,
    Hafez, and seek it while you may,
For lovers will not let the timid
    Amble beside them on love's way.

❧

آنکه رخسار ترا رنگ گل و نسرین داد

THE ONE WHO GAVE YOUR LOVELY FACE ITS ROSY
             red and white
Can give me peace, and patience to endure
             my wretched plight;

The One who taught your curls their airy
             arrogance can give
Me justice to redress the hopeless grief
             in which I live.

Oh, I despaired of Farhad when his hand
             assigned the rein
Of his bewildered heart to Shirin's lips,
             and her disdain.

If treasuries of gold are lacking, well,
             contentment's beckoned;
The One who gives the first to kings sees beggars
             receive the second.

The world displays herself to us as such
             a charming bride,
But life's the dowry that men pay to lie
             at her sweet side.

From now on it's the cypress and the clear
                    streams' banks for me;
Especially now spring's promise scents the breeze
                    incessantly.

"Justice!" I cry. And since, Qavam al-din,
                    we've had to part,
This age's grief, your absent face, usurp
                    Hafez's heart.

یاد باد آنکه نهانت نظری با ما بود

MAY I REMEMBER ALWAYS WHEN
   Your glance in secrecy met mine,
And in my face your love was like
   A visibly reflected sign.

May I remember always when
   Your chiding eyes were like my death
And your sweet lips restored my life
   Like Jesus's reviving breath.

May I remember always when
   We drank our wine as darkness died,
My friend and I, alone at dawn,
   Though God was there too, at our side.

May I remember always when
   Your face was pleasure's flame, and my
Poor fluttering heart was like a moth
   That's singed and is about to die.

May I remember always when
   The company that we were in
Was so polite, and when it seemed
   Only the wine would wink and grin!

May I remember always when
     Our goblet laughed with crimson wine –
What tales passed back and forth between
     Your ruby lips, my dear, and mine!

May I remember always when
     I was a canopy unfurled
That shaded you, and you were like
     The new moon riding through the world.

May I remember always when
     I sat and drank in wine-shops where
What I can't find in mosques today
     Accompanied the drinkers there.

May I remember always when
     The jewels of verse Hafez selected
Were set out properly by you,
     Arranged in order, and corrected.

꙳

واعظان کاین جلوه در محراب و منبر می کنند

THESE PREACHERS WHO MAKE SUCH A SHOW
    Of pulpit piety
Act in a wholly different way
    When no one's there to see.

This is my question for the wise –
    How is it those who teach
Repentance are so rarely found
    To practice what they preach?

You'd think they'd no belief in God
    Or in His Judgment Day,
Given their frauds done in His name,
    The pious tricks they play.

My master reigns among the ruins,
    And the poor whom he
Attracts know needing nothing's wealth,
    And pride's humility.

O God, these nouveaux riches – the slaves
    And mules that they display!
Set them upon their donkeys now,
    And send them on their way!

And angels, say your prayers before
       Love's tavern door – its shade
Is where the clay of Adam's kneaded
       And mankind is made.

His boundless beauty slays the lover,
       And even as he dies,
Out of the darkness, seeking love,
       New multitudes arise.

But hurry, Sufi – in the house
       Where Magians meet they give
The liquid that revives men's hearts
       And makes them truly live.

Empty your house, my heart, so that
       Your Sovereign may preside there,
Since grasping fools despoil both heart
       And soul when they reside there.

At dawn a cry came from the heavens –
       And Reason said, "I see
The very angels know by heart
       Hafez's poetry!"

شکفته شد گل خمری و گشت بلبل مست

THE NIGHTINGALES ARE DRUNK, WINE-RED ROSES APPEAR,
And, Sufis, all around us, happiness is here;

How firmly, like a rock, Repentance stood! Look how
A wine-glass taps it, and it lies in pieces now . . .

Bring wine! From the sequestered court where we're
     secluded,
Drunk or sober, king or soldier, none will be excluded;

This inn has two doors, and through one we have to
     go —
What does it matter if the doorway's high or low?

If there's no sorrow there can be no happiness,
And, when the world was made, men knew this, and
     said, "Yes."

Rejoice, don't fret at Being and Non-Being; say
That all perfection will be nothingness one day.

The horse that rode the wind, Asef in all his glory,
The language of the birds, are now an ancient story;

They've disappeared upon the wind, and Solomon,
The master of them all, has nothing now they've gone.

Don't rise on feathered wings, don't soar into the skies –
An arrow falls to earth, however far it flies;

How will your pen give thanks, Hafez, now men demand
Your verses everywhere, and pass them hand to hand?

مسلمانان مرا وقتی دلی بود

MOSLEMS, TIME WAS I HAD A HEART –

                a good one too,
When problems came we'd talk, and I'd
                know what to do;

And if I tumbled in grief's whirlpool
                my heart was sure
To give me hope that soon enough
                I'd reach the shore –

A sympathetic, generous heart,
                a heart prepared
To help out any noble soul,
                a heart that cared.

This heart was lost to me within
                my lover's street;
God, what a place! – where I succumbed
                to sweet deceit.

There is no faultless art – we all
                fall short somehow,
But what poor beggar's more deprived
                than I am now?

Have pity on this wretched soul
                       and sympathize
With one who once upon a time
                       was strong and wise.

Since love has taught me how to talk,
                       each little phrase
Of mine is cried up everywhere
                       and showered with praise –

But don't call Hafez witty, wise,
                       intelligent;
I've seen Hafez, I know him well;
                       he's ignorant.

باشد ای دل که در میکده ها بکشایند

PERHAPS, MY HEART, THE WINE-SHOPS' DOORS
     will soon be opened wide,
And all the cramping knots in which
     we're tied will be untied;

And if they're closed because of one
     ascetic's canting pride,
Be strong, my heart . . . because of God
     this will be rectified.

I swear by revelers' hearts that those
     who drink at dawn have pried
Apart with prayers so many doors –
     their prayers were satisfied.

Write now the elegy for grape's
     fair child, since she has died!
And make her mourners weep with such
     despair it's blood they've cried.

Sever the harp's strings now in grief
     for wine's cruel homicide;
Likewise the locks of those young boys
     who served wine at our side.

They've closed the wine-shops' doors – ah, God,
      don't let them open wide
The doors to shops whose wares are cant,
      pretentiousness, and pride.

Hafez, this Sufi cloak you wear,
      tomorrow it won't hide
The heathen underneath, and all
      you've claimed will be belied.

ما بدین در نه پی حشمت و جاه آمده ایم

WE HAVEN'T TRAVELED TO THIS DOOR
   For wealth or mastery,
We come here seeking refuge from
   Misfortune's misery.

And we have journeyed all this way,
   Fleeing the confines of
Our Nothingness to seek out Being
   Along the path of love;

From heaven's orchards we have seen
   The springtime of your face,
We traveled here from paradise
   To seek this herb of grace –

For all the treasures Gabriel
   Kept in store for us there,
We've traveled to our Sovereign's door
   Like beggars in despair.

O Holy Ship of Blessings, where
   Is Your strong anchor found?
In sinfulness, within this sea
   Of mercy, we are drowned!

Our good name's gone . . . cover our sins,
   Kind Cloud of Grace – we bring
A blackened record with us to
   The precincts of our King.

Hafez, cast off this Sufi cloak
   And all it signifies –
We've followed here the camel-train
   With ardent, fiery sighs.

گفتم غم تو دارم گفتا غمت سر آید

I SAID, "THE GRIEF I FEEL IS ALL FOR YOU";
                she said, "Your grief will end";
I said, "Be as the moon to me"; she said,
                "That moon might rise, my friend."

I said, "Learn faithfulness from those whose love
                is trustworthy and true";
She said, "That's something moon-like pretty girls
                are rarely known to do."

I said, "I'll bind my eyes up, and I'll keep
                your image from my sight";
She said, "My image is a thief that moves
                invisibly by night."

I said, "Your curls' scent has misled my mind,
                I wander far and wide";
She said, "And when you understand you'll see
                that scent is your true guide."

I said, "Happy the scent from beauty's garden,
                blowing so fresh and sweet";
She said, "Cool is the breeze that blows on us
                from the belovèd's street."

I said, "Wanting to kiss your ruby lips
          has all but murdered me";
She said, "Be as a slave, my lips know how
          to treat slaves lovingly."

I said, "When will your generous heart make peace
          between us – when, my dear?"
She said, "Don't speak of this at all until
          my heart says peace is here."

I said, "And did you see how happiness
          sped by, and could not last?"
She said, "Silence, Hafez; this time of grief
          will also, soon, have passed."

DEAR FRIENDS, THAT FRIEND WITH WHOM WE ONCE
  Caroused at night –
His willing services to us
  And our delight . . . remember this.

And in your joy, when tinkling bells
  And harps are there,
Include within your songs the sound
  Of love's despair . . . remember this.

When wine bestows a smile upon
  Your server's face,
Keep in your songs, for lovers then,
  A special place . . . remember this.

So all that you have hoped for is
  Fulfilled at last?
All that we talked of long ago,
  Deep in the past . . . remember this.

When love is faithful, and it seems
  Nothing can hurt you,
Know that the world is faithless still
  And will desert you . . . remember this.

If Fortune's horse bolts under you,
        Then call to mind
Your riding whip, and see your friends
        Aren't left behind . . . remember this.

O you, who dwell in splendor now,
        Glorious and proud,
Pity Hafez, your threshold's where
        His face is bowed . . . remember this.

شب قدر است وطی شد نامهٔ هجر

IT IS THE NIGHT OF POWER,
　　　　Grief's scroll is rolled away,
Peace to this sacred night
　　　　until the dawning day!

My heart, as you traverse
　　　　love's path, be strong and true –
No step along this way
　　　　will be denied its due.

A libertine is all
　　　　I am, I can't repent –
Although it means that you've
　　　　decreed my banishment.

My heart's gone, and I missed
　　　　the face of its sly thief;
My cries are for my sorrow,
　　　　my sighs are for my grief.

Bring the bright morning to
　　　　my heart, O God; the night
That separation brings
　　　　obliterates my sight.

If you want faith, Hafez,
      put up with faithlessness –
Merchants see loss and profit,
      both failure and success.

ای خرّم از فروغ رخت لالہ زار عمر

LIFE'S GARDEN FLOURISHES WHEN YOUR
　　Bright countenance is here.
Come back! Without your face's bloom
　　The spring has left the year.

If tears course down like raindrops now,
　　It's no surprise, it's right –
My life's flashed by in longing for you
　　As lightning splits the night.

Seize these few moments while we've still
　　Time for our promised meeting,
Since no one knows what life will bring
　　And life, my dear, is fleeting.

How long shall we enjoy our dawns'
　　Sweet sleep, our morning wine?
Wake up, and think of this! Since life's
　　Not yours for long, or mine.

She passed by yesterday, but gave
　　Me not a glance, not one;
My wretched heart, you've witnessed nothing
　　As life's passed by, and gone.

But those whose lives are centered on
       Your lovely mouth confess
No other thoughts than this, and think
       Nothing of Nothingness.

An ambush waits on every side
       Wherever we might tread,
And so life's rider rides slack-reined,
       Giving his horse its head.

I've lived my life without a life –
       Don't be surprised at this;
Who counts an absence as a life
       When life is what you miss?

Speak Hafez! On the world's page trace
       Your poems' narrative;
The words your pen writes will have life
       When you no longer live.

گل عذاری ز گلستان جهان ما را بس

OF ALL THE ROSES IN THE WORLD
   A rosy face . . . is quite enough for me;
Beneath this swaying cypress tree
   A shady place . . . is quite enough for me.

May hypocrites find somewhere else
   To cant and prate –
Of all this weighty world, a full
   Wine-glass's weight . . . is quite enough for me.

They hand out heaven for good deeds!
   The monastery
Where Magians live is better for
   A sot like me . . . that's quite enough for me.

Sit by this stream and watch as life
   Flows swiftly on –
This emblem of the world that's all
   Too quickly gone . . . is quite enough for me.

See how the world's bazaar pays cash,
   See the world's pain –
And if you're not content with this
   World's loss and gain . . . they're quite enough for me.

My friend is here with me – what more
   Should I desire?
The riches of our talk are all
   That I require . . . they're quite enough for me.

Don't send me from your door, O God,
   To paradise –
For me, to wait here at Your street's
   End will suffice . . . that's quite enough for me.

Hafez, don't rail against your fate!
   Your nature flows,
As does your verse, like water as
   It comes and goes . . . that's quite enough for me.

مقام امن و می بی غش و رفیق شفیق

A LOVING FRIEND, GOOD WINE, A PLACE SECURE
                    From enemies –
What luck is yours if you can always lay
                    Your hands on these!

The world, with all its works, amounts to nothing,
                    With naught inside it –
A thousand times I've puzzled over this
                    And verified it.

Alas that I was ignorant till now –
                    But now I'm sure
The alchemy of joy's the friend, the friend
                    And nothing more.

Go somewhere safe, treasure the time you're given,
                    See you enjoy it –
Since bandits lie in wait to snatch your life,
                    And they'll destroy it.

Come now – repentance over ruby lips
                    And wine's red smile
Is just a whim, and one that Reason can't
                    Count as worthwhile.

And if your slender waist's not destined for
                        The likes of me,
I still know happiness when I invoke
                        Its memory;

And then your chin, that's so delectable
                        And sweet I swear
A hundred thousand fancies could not plumb
                        The dimple there . . .

My tears are ruby-red, but that should come
                        As no surprise –
Your lips are ruby-red, it's tears for them
                        That fill my eyes.

He laughed, "Hafez, I am the slave of your
                        Poetic nature –
Look what an utter fool he takes me for,
                        A stupid creature!"

دوش پنهان گفت با من کاردانی تیزهوش

LAST NIGHT THE WINE-SELLER, A MAN
    Of great experience,
Conversed with me (and here I share
    With you his secret sense):

"Go easy on yourself – the world's
    Harsh nature is to be
Hard on the man who's hard upon
    Himself continually."

And then he gave me such a glass
    Of wine its flashing light
Made Venus dance in heaven, and strike
    Her lute in shared delight,

And cry, "Good health!" And he went on:
    "Listen my boy, draw near,
Let sorrow go, take my advice,
    If you have ears to hear;

And if your heart is red with blood,
    Smile as red wine will smile;
Don't cry out like a harp's strings, though
    You're grieving all the while.

Until you pass this veil you can't
      Arrive at what is hidden;
To impure ears Sorush's words
      Must still remain forbidden.

But when it comes to love, life's all
      A listening and a speaking –
We must be then all open eyes
      And ears forever seeking;

And self-promotion's not the mode
      A clever man employs –
Speak if you've knowledge, otherwise
      See that you make no noise!"

Bring wine! Asef, the Lord of Time,
      Who's gracious and forgiving,
Already knows the dissipation
      In which Hafez is living.

راهیست راه عشق که هیچش کناره نیست

LOVE'S ROAD'S AN ENDLESS ROAD
     where there's no place to rest,
Where souls must sacrifice
     themselves, and not protest;

Each moment that you give
     your heart to love is good,
And there's no need to see
     what omens might suggest;

So take the libertine's
     sweet way; not every man
Is shown the road that leads
     to such a treasure chest!

Don't frighten us by saying
     Reason prohibits it;
In our town that police-chief
     has made not one arrest.

Clear eyes can glimpse Him, as
     they glimpse the new moon's sliver,
And not to every gaze
     is this made manifest.

So ask your own eyes then
            just who it is who slays us;
Stars have not sinned here, nor
            have horoscopes transgressed!

Hafez's tears have no
            effect at all; you are
Like granite, as my heart's
            bewilderments attest.

MY HEART, GOOD FORTUNE IS THE ONLY FRIEND
   Going along beside you that you need;
A breeze that's scented with Shiraz's gardens
   Is all the guard to guide you that you need.

Poor wretch, don't leave your lover's home again,
   Don't be in such a hurry to depart –
A corner of our Sufi meeting place,
   The journey in your heart . . . are all you need.

The claims of home, the promises you made
   An ancient friend – these are enough to say
When making your excuses to the travelers
   Who've been along life's way . . . they're all you need.

If grief should leap out from some corner of
   Your stubborn heart and ambush you, confide
Your troubles to our ancient Zoroastrian –
   His precincts will provide . . . you all you need.

Sit yourself down upon the wine-shop's bench
   And take a glass of wine – this is your share
Of all the wealth and glory of the world,
   And what you're given there . . . is all you need.

Let go, and make life easy for yourself,
　　Don't strain and struggle, always wanting more;
A glass of wine, a lover lovely as
　　The moon – you may be sure . . . they're all you need.

The heavens give the ignorant their head,
　　Desire's the only bridle they acknowledge –
Your fault is that you're clever and accomplished,
　　And this same sin of knowledge . . . is all you need.

And you require no other prayer, Hafez,
　　Than that prayed in the middle of the night;
This and the morning lesson you repeat
　　As dawn displays her light . . . are all you need.

Don't look for gifts from others; in both worlds –
　　This world, the world that is to come – your king's
Kind bounty, and the Lord's approval, are
　　The two essential things . . . they're all you need.

گر چه بر واعظ شهر این سخن آسان نشود

ALTHOUGH OUR PREACHER MIGHT NOT LIKE
                    to hear me mention it,
He'll never be a Moslem while
                    he's such a hypocrite.

Learn to be dissolute; be kind –
                    this is far better than
To be a beast that won't drink wine
                    and can't become a man.

The essence must be wholly pure
                    if grace is to be ours;
If not, no stones will turn to pearls,
                    or coral come from flowers.

The Highest will fulfill His aims,
                    rejoice, my heart! No lies
Can make a devil Solomon
                    whatever tricks he tries.

I practice love, a noble trade,
                    and hope that I won't see
Love bring, as other trades have done,
                    sorrow and grief to me.

Last night he said, "Tomorrow I
                    will give you your desire."
O God, don't let regret assail him
                    and make him out a liar!

I'll pray that God adds goodness to
                    the beauty you possess,
So that you'll cease to cause me such
                    distraction and distress.

Hafez, unless a mote aspires
                    and strives, it has no chance
To reach that source from which the sun
                    receives its radiance.

❧

اگر شراب خوری جرعه ای فشان بر خاک

      A few drops on the ground –
What's there to fear from sin
      That spreads such joy around?

Go, drink up all you have,
      Drink now and don't delay –
Death's dagger won't delay
      Dispatching you one day.

My cypress-slender love,
      By the dust on which you tread,
Don't hesitate to visit
      My dust when I am dead.

In heaven or in hell,
      For angels or for men,
In every faith – to hold back
      Counts as a mortal sin.

The Architect of heaven
      Who gave the world its shape
Has sealed its six directions
      So that there's no escape.

The daughter of the vine
      Leads Reason all astray –
May the vine's trellis stand
      Unharmed till Judgment Day!

And may your dear friends' prayers,
      Hafez, when you depart
Via the wine-shop's door,
      Accompany your heart.

دلم ربوده لولی وشیست شورانگیز

MY HEART WAS STOLEN BY A LOUT,
  A gypsy-featured lad
Who broke his promises and was
  Half cut-throat and half mad.

I'd rather see a ripped shirt worn
  By someone blessed with beauty
Than see a thousand Sufi cloaks,
  All abstinence and duty.

An angel has no notion what
  Love is when it's discussed,
No, call for rose water, my boy
  To pour on Adam's dust.

I love the words that kindle fire,
  A verbal conflagration,
Not cold words used to douse the flames
  Of friendly conversation.

I've come now to your court, worn out
  By pain and indigence;
Have mercy on me, I've no hope
  But your benevolence.

Don't put your trust in all the tricks
    And games that you've created;
It's said there are a thousand ways
    For kings to be checkmated.

"Come then," a voice within the wine-shop
    Last night admonished me,
"You've gained contentment, now accept
    This stage as Fate's decree."

Attach a wine-cup to my shroud
    So that on Judgment Day
The wine will help my quaking heart
    Chase all her fears away.

Between the lover and the loved
    There will be no divide,
But you yourself, Hafez, must draw
    The veil of Self aside.

رسید مژده که ایام غم نخواهد ماند

GOOD NEWS! THE DAYS OF GRIEF AND PAIN
                              won't stay like this –
As others went, these won't remain
                    or stay like this.

Though my belovèd thinks of me
                    as dirt and dust,
My rival's status, and her trust,
                    won't stay like this.

And though the doorman wields his sword
                    against us all,
No rank remains immutable
                    or stays like this.

When good or bad come, why give thanks,
                    and why complain?
Since what is written won't remain
                    or stay like this.

They say when Jamshid reigned, "Bring wine"
                    was his court's song,
"Since even Jamshid won't live long,
                    or stay like this."

And if you're wealthy help the poor,

        since, be assured,

The gold and silver that you hoard

        won't stay like this!

O candle, prize the moth's love now

        and hold it fast –

When dawn arrives it cannot last

        or stay like this.

In words of gold they've written on

        the emerald sky,

"Only compassion does not die

        but stays like this."

Do not despair of love, Hafez;

        it can't be true

The heartlessness she's shown to you

        will stay like this.

فاش می گویم و از گفتهٔ خود دلشادم

I'LL SAY IT OPENLY, AND BE
   Happy to speak my mind –
"I am the slave of love, and I
   Have left both worlds behind."

I am a bird from paradise
   And can't account for how
I fell into this trap of troubles
   Where I must languish now.

I was an angel, the highest court
   Of heaven was home to me –
Adam it was who brought me to
   This ruined monastery.

But heavenly shade, the water there,
   The houris' proffered love
Are all forgotten now, and it's
   Your street I'm dreaming of;

And on the tablets of my heart
   My friend's tall stature's written;
What can I do? My master's lesson
   Was this, and now I'm smitten.

No wise astrologer can tell
  What star's assigned to me;
O God, when earth, my mother, bore me,
  What did the heavens decree?

A slave before love's wine-shop door
  Is where and how I live,
And every moment brings to me
  The blessings sorrows give.

My eyes weep heart's blood – this is right
  Given what I have done;
Why did I hand my heart to one
  Beloved by everyone?

Oh, use your hair to wipe the tears
  From your Hafez's face,
Or soon their flood will bear me off
  And leave behind no trace.

حاشا که من به موسم گل ترک می کنم

AH, GOD FORBID THAT I RELINQUISH WINE
When roses are in season;
How could I do this when I'm someone who
Makes such a show of Reason?

Where's a musician, so that I can give
The profit I once found
In self-control and knowledge for a flute's songs,
And a lute's sweet sound?

The endless arguments within the schools –
Whatever they might prove –
Sickened my heart; I'll give a little time
To wine now, and to love.

Where is the shining messenger of dawn
That I might now complain
To my good fortune's harbinger of this
Long night of lonely pain?

But when did time keep faith with anyone?
Bring wine, and I'll recall
The tales of kings, of Jamshid and Kavus,
And how time took them all.

I'm not afraid of sins recorded in
        My name – I'll roll away
A hundred such accounts, by His benevolence
        And grace, on Judgment Day.

This lent soul, that the Friend once gave into
        Hafez's care, I'll place
Within His hands again, on that day when
        I see Him face to face.

صبا به لطف بگو آن غزال رعنا را

MILD BREEZE OF MORNING, GENTLY TELL
   That errant, elegant gazelle
She's made me wander far and wide
   About the hills and countryside.

My sugar-lipped, sweet girl – oh, may
   You live forever and a day! –
Where is your kindness? Come now, show it
   To your sweet-talking parrot-poet.

My rose, does vanity restrain you?
   Does beauty's arrogance detain you
From seeking out this nightingale
   Who wildly sings, to no avail?

With gentleness and kindness lies
   The surest way to win the wise,
Since birds that have become aware
   Of ropes and traps are hard to snare.

When you sit safely with your love,
   Sipping your wine, be mindful of
Those struggling lovers who still stray,
   Wind-tossed, upon their weary way.

I don't know why she isn't here,
   Why her tall presence won't appear,
Or why the full moon of her face,
   And her black eyes, avoid this place.

No fault can be imputed to
   Your beauty's excellence, or you,
Except that there is not a trace
   Of truth or kindness in your face.

When Hafez speaks, it's no surprise
   If Venus dances in the skies
And leads across the heavens' expanse
   Lord Jesus in the whirling dance.

مژدهٔ وصل تو کو کز سر جان برخیزم

WHERE IS THE NEWS WE'LL MEET, THAT FROM
    This life to greet you there   I may arise?
I am a bird from paradise,
    And from this world's cruel snare   I will arise.

Now by my love for you, I swear
    That if you summon me
To be your slave, from all existence
    And its sovereignty   I will arise.

O Lord, make rain fall from Your cloud
    Sent to us as a guide,
Send it before, like scattered dust
    That's wind-blown far and wide,   I will arise.

Sit by my dust with wine and music:
    From my imprisonment
Beneath the ground, within my grave,
    Dancing, drawn by your scent,   I will arise.

Rise now, my love, display your stature,
    Your sweetness, and I'll be,
Like Hafez, from the world itself
    And from my soul set free . . .   I will arise.

And though I'm old, if you'll embrace
   Me tightly in your arms all night,
Then from your side, as dawn appears,
   Young in the morning light,   I will arise.

من دوستدار روی خوش و موی دلکشم

MY LOVE'S FOR PRETTY FACES,
    For heart-bewitching hair;
I'm crazy for good wine,
    A languorous, drunk stare . . .

In love there's no escaping
    The burning of desire;
I stand here like a candle –
    Don't scare me with your fire.

I am a man from heaven,
    But on this path I see
My love of youth and beauty
    Have made a slave of me.

If Fate will help me, I
    Will take myself elsewhere –
My bed will be swept clean
    By some sweet houri's hair.

Shiraz is like a mine
    Of ruby lips, a store
Of loveliness . . . and I'm
    A jeweler who's dirt-poor.

I've seen so many drunk
  Eyes in this town, I think
I'm drunk, although I swear
  I've had no wine to drink.

You asked me to explain
  Eternity for you –
Well certainly, when I
  Have downed a drink or two.

Hafez, my nature's like
  A hopeful bride, but I
Lack mirrors to array
  Myself – that's why I sigh.

مجاب چهرهٔ جان می‌شود غبار تنم

MY BODY'S DUST IS AS A VEIL
  Spread out to hide
My soul – happy that moment when
  It's drawn aside!

To cage a songbird with so sweet
  A voice is wrong –
I'll fly to paradise's garden
  Where I belong.

But why I've come and whence I came
  Is all unclear –
Alas, to know so little of
  My being here!

How can I make my journey to
  My heavenly home
When I'm confined and cramped within
  This flesh and bone?

If my blood smells of longing, show no
  Astonishment –
Mine is the musk deer's pain as he
  Secretes his scent.

Don't think my golden shirt is like
   A candle's light –
The true flame burns beneath my shirt,
   Hidden from sight.

Come, and ensure Hafez's being
   Will disappear –
Since You exist, no one will hear
   Me say, "I'm here."

نفس باد صبا مشک فشان خواهد شد

THE MUSKY MORNING BREEZE
  Will gently blow again,
Once more the old world will
  Turn young and grow again;

White jasmine will take wine
  From glowing Judas trees,
Narcissi fondly glance
  At shy anemones;

Once more the banished, lovelorn
  Nightingale will bring
His passion to the rose
  And there sublimely sing;

And if I leave the mosque
  For wine, don't sneer at me –
Sermons are long, and time
  Moves on incessantly.

My heart, if you postpone
  Today's enjoyment, who
Will guarantee the cash
  Of happiness to you?

Drink before fasting, drink,
   Don't put your glass down yet –
Since Ramadan draws near
   And pleasure's sun must set.

How sweet the roses are!
   Enjoy them now, for they
As quickly as they bloomed
   Will fall and fade away.

We're all friends here, my boy,
   Sing love songs! Why should you
Sing yet again, "As that
   Has gone, so this must too"?

You are why Hafez lives –
   But now, within your heart,
Prepare to say farewell,
   Since he too must depart.

❧

اگر آن ترک شیرازی به دست آرد دل ما را

IF THAT SHIRAZI TURK WOULD TAKE
  My heart within his loving hand
I'd give for his dark mole the towns
  Of Bokhara and Samarqand;

Come boy, and pour the wine's last drops –
  Since heaven's courts will not provide
The gardens of our Mosalla
  Or Roknabad's green riverside.

Alas, these rowdy, sweet-voiced gypsies
  Have ripped out patience from my heart,
Like Turks who make off with a feast's
  Leftovers when the guests depart.

My friend's great beauty has no need
  Of a defective love like mine -
A lovely face does not require
  Cosmetic arts to make it shine.

Let's talk of wine and music, not
  Of Fate, and how the heavens revolve -
Theirs is a riddle no man's wisdom
  Has solved yet, or will ever solve.

Given the beauty Joseph had
    I understood love could not fail
To tempt Zuleikha to discard
    Her chastity's enclosing veil.

You slandered me, and you spoke well –
    May God forgive you what you said!
A bitter answer suits such lips,
    So sugar-sweet and ruby-red.

But listen to advice, my dear -
    Those who are young and fortunate
Prefer the wisdom of the old
    To their own souls' uncertain state.

Hafez, your poem's written now,
    The pearl you've pierced is poetry's;
Sing sweetly – heaven grants your verse
    The necklace of the Pleiades.

❧

عشق بازیّ و جوانی و شراب لعل فام

FLIRTATIOUS GAMES, AND YOUTH,
   And wine like rubies glowing;
Convivial company,
   And drink that's always flowing;

A sweet-mouthed boy to serve
   And sweet-voiced singers too,
An elegant, dear friend
   Who's seated next to you;

A kindly youngster whose
   Delightful purity
Would stir the Fount of Youth
   To angry jealousy –

A stealer of men's hearts
   Whose charm and loveliness
Would make the moon herself
   Turn pale and envious;

A meeting place as though
   Heaven's high courts surround us,
With paradise's roses
   Profusely growing round us;

Kind-hearted friends to drink with,
    Servants who act discreetly,
Companions who keep secrets,
    Whom we can trust completely;

With wine as red as roses,
    Astringent, light to sip,
Whose tale is garnets, rubies,
    Kissed in a lover's lip;

The server's glance to be
    A sword to plunder reason,
The lovers' curls like snares
    To trip hearts with their treason;

A wit like Hafez, all
    Sweet-talk and repartee,
A patron like Qavam,
    Whose generosity

Lights up the world . . . and may
    The man who turns away
From pleasures such as these
    Not know one happy day!

چون جامه ز تن برکشد آن مشکین خال

A BLACK MOLE GRACED HIS FACE; HE STRIPPED, AND SHONE
Incomparable in splendor as the moon;
He was so slim his heart was visible,
As if clear water sluiced a granite stone.

⁏

عمری زپی مراد ضایع دارم

DESIRE'S DESTROYED MY LIFE; WHAT GIFTS HAVE I
Been given by the blindly turning sky?
And, such is my luck, everyone I said
"Dear friend" to loathed me by and by.

⁏

من حاصل عمرخود ندارم جز غم

WHAT DOES LIFE GIVE ME IN THE END BUT SORROW?
What do love's good and evil send but sorrow?
I've only seen one true companion – pain,
And I have known no faithful friend but sorrow.

⁏

هر دوست که دم زد ز وفا دشمن شد

EACH FRIEND TURNED OUT TO BE AN ENEMY,
Corruption rotted all their "purity";
They say the night is pregnant with new times,
But since no men are here, how can that be?

با مَی به کنار جوی می باید بود

WITH WINE BESIDE A GENTLY FLOWING BROOK – THIS IS BEST;
Withdrawn from sorrow in some quiet nook – this is best;
Our life is like a flower's that blooms for ten short days,
Bright laughing lips, a friendly fresh-faced look – this is best.

Jahan Malek Khatun

For most of these long nights I stay awake
And go to bed as dawn begins to break;
I think that eyes that haven't seen their friend
Might get some sleep then . . . this is a mistake.

تو تا کی همچو سرو از ما کشی سر

HOW LONG WILL YOU BE LIKE
   A cypress tree,
And lean your lovely head
   Away from me?

Sorrow is all you've ever
   Brought to me;
I will not ask how long
   I am to be

The knocker on your door
   You do not see,
The iron ring you pass
   Obliviously.

My pillow's made of absence –
   While you are free
To taste another's love,
   Forgetting me.

If I could follow your
   Curls' scent I'd see
A way to let their night
   Envelop me;

Since you have left me to
    This misery,
Tears, and a heart on fire
    Are all of me.

I don't deserve you, but
    I long to see
The sunlight of your face
    Shine here, for me.

Although you've shown that you
    Don't care for me,
My soul still wishes you
    Prosperity.

الٰہی تو بکشا دری از بہشت

O GOD, I BEG YOU, OPEN WIDE
   The gates of heaven
For one to whom a heavenly nature
   Had been given;

Grant her a place in paradise,
   And may the throngs
Of lovely houris welcome her
   Where she belongs;

Keep far from her this world's desires,
   Its grief and spite;
Bestow your grace on her, and fill
   Her soul with light.

❧

هر که که گلی تازه به صبحم بنمود

EACH NEW FLOWER OPENING IN THE MORNING LIGHT,
Filling my heart with glory and delight . . .
Even before its perfume reaches me
Destruction's wind has swept it from my sight.

❧

با درد تو درمان نپذیرد دل من

MY HEART WILL TAKE NO DRUG TO DULL THIS PAIN,
The seal of Sorrow's set, and will remain:
My heart could never tire of your sweet presence,
Absence is all my life can now contain.

❧

Jahan Malek Khatun • *139*

در جوانی قدر خود نشناختم

I DIDN'T KNOW MY VALUE THEN, WHEN I
   Was young, so long ago;
And now that I have played my part out here,
   What is it that I know?

I know that, now that both of them have gone,
   Life's good and bad passed by
As quickly in my youth as dawn's first breeze
   Forsakes the morning sky.

How many ardent birds of longing then
   Were lured down from the air
By my two ringlets' curls and coils, to be
   Held trapped and helpless there!

And in youth's lovely orchard then I raised
   My head as prettily,
As gracefully, above the greensward there,
   As any cypress tree;

Until, with charming partners to oppose me,
   I took up lovers' chess,
And lost so many of love's pieces to
   My partners' handsomeness –

And then how often on the spacious field
 Of beauty I urged on
My hopeful heart's untiring steed, always
 Pursuing what was gone.

Now, as no shoots or leaves remain to me
 From youth, and youth's delight,
I fit myself in my old age to face
 The darkness of the night.

دلا در باغ حسنش عندلیبم

HEART, IN HIS BEAUTY'S GARDEN, I —
  Like nightingales — complain,
And of his roses now for me
  Only the thorns remain;

My friends have gathered flowers, but I,
  Because of all his harshness,
Can find no flowers to gather here
  And search for them in vain.

My heart is filled with suffering;
  And all my doctor says is,
"Sugar from him, and nothing else,
  Will lessen your heart's pain."

I've filled the world with love for him,
  So why do I receive
Such cruelty from my dearest love,
  Again, and yet again?

My free will's gone from me, so how
  Can my poor ears accept
All the advice my clever tutor's
  Homilies contain?

No, in the pre-dawn darkness, I
   Am like the nightingale
That in the orchards sings the rose
   Its old love-sick refrain.

I hear it's strangers whom you welcome,
   Whom you make much of now;
Let me then be a stranger in
   The kingdom where you reign.

گرم بوسی دهی از لعل پرنوش

IF YOU SHOULD KISS ME WITH
   Your ruby lips, my dear,
I'd be your slave and wear
   Your earring in my ear.

Who has such lovely eyes,
   Or lips, or cheeks, as you?
Who has your hair, your neck,
   Or your complexion? Who?

Who's seen a moon wear such
   A hat? And who is there
Who's seen a cypress tree
   Wrapped in the cloak you wear?

O God, give me the rose
   And not the thorns of love;
O God, don't nip me with
   Those lips I'm dreaming of.

I'm like a cooking pot
   That's placed upon love's fire –
All day and night I seethe
   And bubble with desire;

I've cried too much since you've
        Been absent from my sight;
What do you know of all
        That I endured last night?

Why have you hurt my heart
        With grief, so callously?
And what's made you forget
        Your promises to me?

دلم همچو سر زلفست درهم

MY HEART IS TANGLED LIKE THICK CURLS
  And no one hears me grieve;
In all the world I've no friend since
  You said you had to leave.

What will become of this poor wretch
  With no friend at her side,
With no one but her own despair
  In whom she can confide?

Tell me about his eyes and heart –
  Absence, give me his news,
Pour out the wine now, glass by glass;
  Pour for me, don't refuse.

Your leaving is a sword that's pierced
  My memory; ah, give
The balm of your return to me,
  Quickly, and let me live.

You know your kindness, O my love,
  And it alone will burn,
In all the world, my aching heart
  For good and bad in turn.

O God, why have You made my back
  Bow down beneath the weight
Of his long absence? Why have You
  Reduced me to this state?

The stream that flows within this garden
  Says to the cypress tree,
"May God forbid your shade should ever
  Diminish over me!"

I didn't start this love that makes
  Me suffer so, and grieve;
These games of love were started first
  When Adam sinned with Eve.

صبا بازآ که در مانم تو داری

SWEET BREEZE RETURN TO ME, YOU BEAR
The scent of my belovèd's hair.

I suffered while you were away;
You'll bring the balm for my despair.

My doctors are so sick of all
My sicknesses; but I know where

The medicine lies – it's in the scent
You'll bring to me from his sweet hair.

Tell him, "I'm half insane without you,
You'll cure these pains I cannot bear."

Don't say to him, "How long, my love,
Will you condemn me to despair?"

❦

ای برده آتش رخ تو آب و رنگ گل

YOUR FACE USURPS THE FIERY GLOW AND HUE
                              of roses;
And with your face here, what have I to do
                              with roses?

Your ringlets' fragrance is so sweet, my friend,
No fragrant rose-scent could entice me to
                              seek roses –

Besides, the faithless roses' scent will fade,
Which is a serious drawback, in my view,
                              of roses;

And if the waters of eternal life
Had touched their roots, so that they bloomed anew,
                              these roses,

When could they ever form a bud as sweet
As your small mouth, which is more trim and true
                              than roses?

❦

عهد کردم که ازین پس نه هم دل به خیال

FROM NOW ON I HAVE SWORN
  I won't let dreams deceive me,
Since pointless dreams have made
  My spirit almost leave me;

My poor heart dreamed of you
  So earnestly it seems,
Your image turned my flesh
  Into the stuff of dreams.

I gave my head, heart, soul,
  And faith to you – so who
Informed you killing me's
  A legal thing to do?

Have mercy on me now,
  Pity my wretchedness,
I've reached the limits of
  Exhaustion and distress.

Now by his doe-like eyes,
  The full moon of his face,
His eyebrow's arch that's like
  The new moon in its grace,

By his bright cheeks, the rose
   And jasmine mingled there,
By his moist lips, and by
   The sweet scent of his hair,

By my parched, thirsty lips,
   By meeting him at night,
By his proud stride, and by
   His sapling-slender height,

I swear that in this night
   Of his long absence, my
Poor face is pallid as
   The pale moon in the sky;

I swear that I despair
   Of heart and soul, and of
Both this world and the next,
   Without him, and his love.

"You're like the nightingale,"
   He said, "whose lovesick woe
Harangues the rose! Poor wretch,
   Stop whining now, and go!"

خوابی خوش است اینکه شب دوش دیده ام

HOW SWEET SLEEP IS! I DREAMED I SAW
  My friend last night,
And pampered my poor heart with thoughts
  Of past delight;

And in this dream he was so kind
  And sweet to me,
I entertain high hopes that this
  Is how he'll be . . .

I saw your lovely face, and what
  Could be more clear
In meaning than that I should see
  Your face appear?

Be chivalrous and kind to me –
  Have pity on
One who has suffered agonies
  Since you have gone:

I'm like a cypress who has bowed
  Her stately grace
Down to the earth in searching for
  Your flower-like face;

I long so much to see you here,
    Each night I tear
A hundred nightshirts into shreds
    In my despair.

You are the ka'abah that I seek:
    My love, allow
Me to approach the face I've sought
    For so long now.

I'm like a bird that is half slaughtered,
    Struggling to rise,
Whose wings are dabbled with her heart's
    Blood as she dies.

I know too well the warmth and cold
    That Fortune's shown;
I'm not a child to whom the world
    Is still unknown.

بیا بنشین مرو در خواب امشب

COME HERE A MOMENT, SIT WITH ME, DON'T SLEEP TONIGHT,
Consider well my heart's unhappy plight, tonight;

And let your face's presence lighten me, and give
The loveliness of moonlight to the night, tonight.

Be kind now to this stranger, and don't imitate
Life as it leaves me in its headlong flight, tonight.

Be sweet to me now as your eyes are sweet; don't twist
Away now like your curls, to left and right, tonight;

Don't sweep me from you like the dust before your door;
Dowse all the flames of longing you ignite, tonight.

Why do you treat me with such cruelty now, my friend,
So that my tears obliterate my sight, tonight?

If, for a moment, I could see you in my dreams,
I'd know the sum of all this world's delight, tonight.

❧

بگو چگونه دهم شرح آرزومندی

When you'll be angry with me if I do?

Your slave is guilty; would it hurt to show
Her kindness, though? Noblesse oblige, you know.

My heart and soul are yours now; in which case,
Tell me, why slam your door shut in my face?

Don't hurt my heart like this . . . because I bet
If this were done to you, you'd be upset!

My heart, the man's a cad; so how's his hair
Managed to tangle you within its snare?

How you hung on to love! And now the fire
Of his long absence burns me with desire.

Men love the world, she's dear to everyone –
So why's the world's love something that you shun?

🍃

بہ باغ شد دل من صبحدم بہ گل چیدن

AT DAWN MY HEART SAID I SHOULD GO
  Into the garden where
I'd pick fresh flowers, and hope to see
  His flower-like beauty there.

I took his hand in mine, and oh
  How happily we strayed
Among the tulip beds, and through
  Each pretty grassy glade;

How sweet the tightness of his curls
  Seemed then, and it was bliss
To grasp his fingers just as tight,
  And snatch a stealthy kiss.

For me to be alone beside
  That slender cypress tree
Cancels the thousand injuries
  That he has given me.

He's a narcissus, tall and straight!
  And so how sweet to bow
My head like violets at his feet
  And kiss the earth there now.

But your drunk eyes don't deign to see me,
   Although I really think
It's easy to forgive someone
   The worse for love or drink.

And though it's good to weep beneath
   God's cloud of clement rain,
It's also good to laugh like flowers
   When sunlight shines again.

My heart was hurt by his "Checkmate";
   I think I must prepare
To seek out wider pastures then,
   And wander off elsewhere.

Jahan, be careful not to say
   Too much; it's pitiful
To give a jewel to someone who
   Can't see it's valuable.

گر آید نسیمی ز سوی نگار

SUPPOSE A BREEZE SHOULD BRING TO ME
  My lover's scent –
I'd sacrifice my heart and soul
  And be content;

My nostrils would inhale his scent
  And be at rest
Since by the breezes of the spring
  The world is blessed.

And spring is here, the New Year's here,
  And brings to me
A fragrance that's like pungent musk
  From Tartary;

What camphor, musk, and ambergris
  Are mingled there
So that the scent resembles now
  My lover's hair.

If he should wander through these gardens,
  Shame would make
Each rose shed all its petals for
  His beauty's sake;

And shameful of their stature, elms
  Would watch him pass,
And Oriental planes bow down
  And touch the grass;

And violets would be ashamed
  To see his hair –
They'd wilt away beneath his steps
  In their despair;

Narcissi, with their drunken eyes,
  Before his feet
Would bow their heads and, as they bowed,
  Admit defeat.

The blossoms of the Judas tree
  Would blush for shame,
Sweet-smelling lilies would heap praise
  Upon his name;

And jessamine that loves to boast
  Of its fair face
Would die upon his roses' thorns
  And cede its place;

The splendid tulips would turn pale,
    And everywhere
No rose or jasmine would be looked at
    While he was there.

And in each place, throughout the garden,
    A thousand cries
Like drunken shouts, in praise of him,
    Would then arise.

Now, in this season of spring flowers,
    I long to be
Surrounded by them, with my lover
    Seated with me,

With blossoms drifting down on us,
    As though the sweet
Flowers falling were a silver tribute
    Cast at his feet.

The world is filled with happiness;
    But no relief
Is mine, since in these days I know
    Nothing but grief.

الٰهی تو بکشا بلطفت دری

O GOD, BE KIND, AND OPEN WIDE YOUR DOOR,
I don't want others' kindness any more;

And if I've strayed from the right path, I know
That You will guide me where I have to go

(If He considers me at all, then I
Will gladly give my soul for Him, and die);

All powerful God, who needs no human prayer,
Open Your door to me, receive me there.

In one night, sovereignty abandoned me –
Your kindness now is all my sovereignty.

And who dare praise You or extol You? Who,
For all his eloquence, can speak of You?

If You're my friend, then what is it to me
If all my country's now my enemy?

🦋

یاری که همه میل دلش سوی وفا بود

MY FRIEND, WHO WAS SO KIND AND FAITHFUL ONCE,
Has changed his mind now, and I don't know why;

I think it must be in my wretched stars –
He feels no pity for me when I cry.

Oh, I complain of your cruel absence, but
Your coming here's like dawn's breeze in the sky;

That oath you swore to and then broke – thank God
It's you who swore, and is foresworn, not I!

I didn't snatch one jot of joy before
You snatched your clothes from me and said goodbye;

I didn't thank you, since I wasn't sure
You'd really been with me, or just passed by.

How envious our clothes were when we lay
Without them, clasped together, you and I!

Your curls have chained my heart up; this is right –
Madmen are chained up, as they rage and sigh.

They say the world's lord cherishes his slaves;
So why's he harsh to me? I don't know why.

❦

Faces of Love • *162*

HAVE ALL YOUR FEELINGS FOR ME GONE?
Tell me, how long must this go on?
Who snatched my heart from me but you?
Dearest, is this what lovers do?

My love, you loved me once, and how
Am I to bear this anguish now?
You stole my heart, and now your prey's
My soul . . . these are not friendship's ways!

As lion-hunting kings pursue
Their prey across the plain, so you
Have killed my heart – that is now tied
As spoils hung from your saddle's side.

My weeping was the rain whose power
Nourished this world-destroying flower
That gives me only thorns; O you,
My heart, what can, what will, you do?

❦

عاقبت کار فروبستہ خدا بکشاید

IT WILL BE GOD WHO OPENS UP,
At last, these bonds that hamper me,

Who in His mercy opens wide,
For me, the door of Victory.

Don't grieve, my heart; His kindness will
Undo the knots entangling me.

It's useless to petition people –
It's God who grants us sovereignty;

My pain has passed all limits, but
His mercy is its remedy.

Open that door of Victory,
Dear God! Who else will succor me?

But in the night of loneliness,
Until its long anxiety

Resolves at last, the wretched heart
Must learn to suffer patiently.

O world, the heavens have chained your feet,
Your shackles are their tyranny –

Pray now that, by prayer's influence,
They'll open up, and you'll be free.

❦

یاد باد آنکه عزیزان همه باهم بودیم

HOW SWEET THOSE DAYS WHEN WE WERE STILL
        together; when we cared
For one another, and our grief
        and happiness were shared!

We used no waspish tongues to wound
        each other's hearts; we swore
That we'd be one another's shields,
        faithful for evermore!

And would, thanks be to God, be famed
        for how much we'd dispense
In charity, and for our buildings'
        bold magnificence.

For years we took our pleasure, laughed
        aloud – it was as though
We were spring flowers, and happiness
        was all that we could know;

And we were kind, considerate,
                     politely intimate –
As gentle as the morning breeze
                     with every soul we met.

We spread our light throughout the world
                     as if we were the sun,
And like the sun itself we dried
                     dew's tears for everyone.

جانا چه باشد ار دل ما را دوا کنی

HOW WOULD IT BE, MY SOUL'S LOVE, IF YOU HEALED
      My heart for me,
And pitied my poor state, and didn't stay
      Apart from me?

Your ruby lips are fire, your face is like
      The shining moon;
It would be right for you to visit me,
      My dear, and soon.

You swore a thousand times you'd come, which you
      Have not yet done –
Of all the promises you've made, why don't
      You keep just one?

I have endured a wretched lifetime of
      Your tyranny;
Tell me, my dear, how long will you go on
      Tormenting me?

How often will you swear to me, "I'll come"
      And then desert me?
Your leaving me's a brand – how long do you
      Intend to hurt me?

Why do you injure all your friends like this
        Continually?
And make me into what my enemies
        Would wish for me?

My heart, how long will all this longing last?
        Calm down, and rest;
You'll certainly upset the world if you
        Don't stop this quest!

به عالم غیر تو یاری ندارم

IN ALL THE WORLD, MY LOVE,
I've no one else but you;
And loving your dear face
I've nothing else to do.

You might have other loves
In place of me, but I,
I swear by your sweet soul,
Have no one else but you.

Dogs haunt the alley where
You live, so why, my friend,
Am I forbidden now
To haunt your alley too?

You are my lord, and I'm
Your slave – command me then;
I promise you I won't
Be angry if you do;

And if I've been upset
And hurt in former days,
I'm never now upset,
My only love, with you.

I swear, from all the earth,
And from its loves, I want
Your kindness – nothing else;
My only lord is you.

چرا به کار من ناتوان نپردازی

WHY IS IT YOU NEGLECT ME SO? WHY IS IT
You never pay your captive wretch a visit?
Your rank's raised your pavilion up to heaven,
Our government's the playground you've been given;
Iran's wealth's lifted you aloft – it's right
Her crown and throne afford you such delight.
Thank God for pleasure, for such luxuries
Snatched at in ever greater quantities!

The world's deceived you for five days, and you're
So proud? It's done this countless times before.
Mohammad Ghazi, in your reign I'm free
Of hearth and home, and all that's dear to me;
But you'll be humbled by the world's attacks,
In sorrow's flames you'll writhe like melting wax.

❧

بیشتر خلق جهان در پی جاه و درمند

MOST PEOPLE IN THE WORLD WANT POWER AND MONEY,
And just these two; that's all they're looking for.
They're faithless, callous, and unkind – the times
Are filled with squabbles, insurrections, war,
And everyone puts caution first, since now
Few friends exist of whom one can be sure.

Men flee from one another like scared deer,
And for a bit of bread the rabble roar
As though they'd tear each other's guts apart.
And why are men determined to ignore
The turning of the heavens, which must mean
The world will change, as it has done before?

But in their souls they are Your slaves, and search
The meadows for the cypress they adore;
My heart's an untamed doe, who haunts Your hills,
And whom no noose has ever snared before.

❧

تا به چند آن غمزه از من دلربایی می کند

HIS GLANCES TRAP MY HEART WITHIN THEIR SNARE,
And straightaway his glances stray elsewhere;

He is the brightness of my eyes, so why
Should he light others' eyes up over there?

I've loved him faithfully for years; but he's
Habitually unfaithful everywhere.

In all the world, no heart is safe from him,
There's not a single heart he'd care to spare!

My fortune led me to delusion's garden,
And all that scoundrel said was, "I don't care."

The day we met I gave my soul to him.
And why? To have him leave me in despair?

The heart's the body's queen; and look, my love,
At your street's end – a queen stands begging there.

❦

WHY, IN YOUR HEART, HAVE YOU FORGOTTEN ME
And put your loving arms round someone new?

You think that I don't know these things? My dear,
My eyes and ears are always close to you.

Forgetting friends is not how friends behave –
It isn't manly, doing what you do!

Why do you veil your face from me, my friend?
A fire's not normally kept out of view.

I burn with longing – come to me, my love;
Bees sting, but then they give us honey too.

Jahan is ready to give up the ghost;
How long must she be silent, missing you?

He said, "Absence is bitter, but your glass
Contains it; drink – swallow the residue!"

نگارا ‌سم دلداری نداری

YOU DON'T KNOW HOW YOU OUGHT TO TREAT A LOVER,
Not for a moment do you think of me;
My heart is broken, and it won't recover,
Since you won't show me any sympathy.

Your only way is to be pitiless,
Your only path's the path of tyranny;
You don't acknowledge my long faithfulness
Since you've no interest in fidelity.

You spend all night asleep or drunk, and give
No thought at all to sleepless, weeping, me –
And what use are my tears, since all you live
For's to be spiteful and act thoughtlessly?

I didn't know that when you swore your oath
Your "Yes" was all that I was going to hear;
You don't care for Jahan, while I gave both
My world and soul into your hands, my dear.

Submit, my heart, and learn to tolerate
This grief, since you will find no other fate.

به رخ چون ماه تابانی به قد چون سرو آزادی

YOUR FACE IS LIKE A SHINING SUN,
   your stature's like a cypress tree
That grows in paradise, and I'm
   your slave; I've no wish to be free.

Be just to me, my love; from your
   bright day bestow one night on me;
If you're unjust, be fearful of
   my groans, my wails of misery.

My heart is in my mouth, because
   of you my soul's about to flee,
So tell me, what makes you, my dear,
   so happy and so contrary?

My lovely moon, my heart has borne
   for you such endless agony;
Why must you brand my breast again
   with absence, with your leaving me?

هنوز از بادهٔ وصل تو مستم

I AM STILL DRUNK THAT YOU WERE HERE,
                            and you were mine,
And once again I stretch my hand out
                        for that wine;

As your drunk eyes could not bestir
                            themselves, I too
Can't move; as you love wine, I love
                        the wine that's you;

And I will ask the gentle morning
                        breeze to bear
A message to my love who has
                        such musky hair,

Since that black hair's sweet scent, from being
                        next to me,
Has made me like a musk deer come
                        from Tartary.

I fainted when you were not here,
                        I could not stand –
Be with me now, my love, support me,
                        grasp my hand;

Oh, I was so distracted, heart-sick,
                  that I gave
My soul into your ringlets' snare,
                  I was your slave;

My eyes wept tears of blood while you
                  were never there,
My feet were shackled in your curls'
                  enclosing snare.

How sad my heart was then! But, God
                  be praised, relief
Has now arrived for me; I have
                  escaped from grief!

ای که پنداری که ما را جز تو یاری هست نیست

I KNOW YOU THINK THAT THERE ARE OTHER FRIENDS FOR ME THAN YOU:
                                        Not so.
And that apart from loving you I've other things to do:
                                        Not so.

Belovèd, out of pity, take my hand before I fall;
You think the world can give me other loves to cling on to?
                                        Not so.

You strike me like a harp, play on me like a flute – and now
You have the nerve to claim that I have had enough of you?
                                        Not so.

What heavy sorrows weigh me down, and crush my abject soul –
Could anything be harder than your absence to live through?
                                        Not so.

Your eyes are languorous and rob my wakeful eyes of sleep,
Are any curls as wild as yours, as lovely and untrue?
                                        Not so.

You say my heart has not been hurt by your disdain. It has.
Has any lover suffered love's despair as I do now for you?
                                        Not so.

You have so many slaves, all finer than I am, I know –
But can you point to one more wretched in your retinue?
                                        Not so.

❧

Jahan Malek Khatun • *179*

این جور و جفای چرخ تا چند

HOW LONG WILL HEAVEN'S HEARTLESS TYRANNY
Which keeps both rich and poor in agony

Go on? The dreadful happenings of these times
Have torn up by the roots Hope's noble tree,

And in the garden of the world you'd say
They've stripped the leaves as far as one can see.

That cypress which was once the cynosure
Of souls, they've toppled ignominiously;

I cry to heaven above, again I cry,
How long will this injustice fall on me?

What can I tell my grieving heart that won't
Let dearest friends assuage its misery?

You'd say heaven's stuffed its ears with scraps of cotton
Simply to show that it's ignoring me!

دوش در خواب چنان دید دو چشم بختم

<small>LAST NIGHT I DREAMED I SAW WITH FORTUNE'S EYES</small>
The garden of my hopes revive its reign;

Its flowers all opened, and my foes departed,
And all my friends sat with me once again.

My moon of hope was full (although in truth
The darkness of these skies has made her wane);

I thanked God for my fortune, and I said,
"My heart's been granted all she'd hoped to gain."

گل رفت و وداع گل زجان باید کرد

<small>THE ROSES HAVE ALL GONE; "GOODBYE," WE SAY; WE MUST;</small>
And I shall leave the busy world one day; I must.
My little room, my books, my love, my sips of wine –
All these are dear to me; they'll pass away; they must.

به کنج مدرسه‌ای کز دلم خرابتر است

HERE, IN THE CORNER OF A RUINED SCHOOL
(More ruined even than my heart), I wait

While men declare that there's no goodness in me.
I sit alone, and brood upon my fate,

And hear their words, like salt rubbed in my wounds,
And tell myself I must accept my state:

I don't want wealth, and I don't envy them
The ostentatious splendor of the great.

What do they want from me, though, since I've
    nothing?
Now that I'm destitute, and desolate?

❦

گفتم که دگر چشم به دلبر نکنم

I SWORE I'D NEVER LOOK AT HIM AGAIN,
I'd be a Sufi, deaf to sin's temptations;
I saw my nature wouldn't stand for it –
From now on I renounce renunciations.

❦

در باغ برهنه گشتی ای شاهد شنگ

YOU WANDERED THROUGH MY GARDEN, NAKED AND ALONE
(The roses blenched to see their beauty overthrown).
My cheeky love, your body is the Fount of Youth
(But in your silver breast your heart is like a stone).

🦋

در دیده خیال تست ما را همه جا

WHEREVER MY EYES LOOK I SEE YOUR IMAGE THERE,
And fears of your departure fill me with despair:
Your face before me tells me to be patient – but
Here is my heart, and – tell me – where is patience? Where?

🦋

من دوش قضا یار و قدر پشتم بود

LAST NIGHT, MY LOVE, MY LIFE, YOU LAY WITH ME,
I grasped your pretty chin, I fondled it,
And then I bit, and bit, your sweet lips till
I woke . . . It was my fingertip I bit.

🦋

مشکل که به درد عشق در مانم نیست

MY LOVE'S AN ACHE NO OINTMENTS CAN ALLAY NOW;
My soul's on fire – how long you've been away now!
I said, "I will be patient while he's gone."
(But that's impossible . . . it's one whole day now . . .)

🦋

ای دل ستم از یار جفا پیشه بسیست

I TOLD MY HEART, "I CAN'T ENDURE THIS TYRANNY!
He's nothing, no one! What's this bully's love to me?"
My little heart, you're like a boundless sea, it seems;
And common sense? A splinter somewhere on that sea.

❦

ای دل بنشین و با غم یار بساز

MY HEART, SIT DOWN, WELCOME LOVE'S PAIN,
                    and make the best of it:
The rose is gone, the thorns remain,
                    so make the best of it.
My heart said, "No! I can't endure
                    this sadness any longer . . . "
I said, "You've no choice – don't complain,
                    just make the best of it."

❦

بر درد دلم طبیب ارا گاه شود

I FEEL SO HEART-SICK. SHOULD MY DOCTOR HEAR,
He'll sigh and groan and want to interfere:
Come on now dearest, heal me, you know how
To make my doctor's headache disappear.

زدم ز فراق روی دلدار چو شمع

YOUR FACE'S ABSENCE LEAVES MINE WAXY-WHITE,
                              like a candle;
How long will my tears drip, blearing my sight,
                              like a candle?
You sleep, and on your pillow I lie broken,
                              self-consumed,
Awake and weeping till the morning light,
                              like a candle.

پروانه صفت پیش تو در پروازم

I'M LIKE THE MOTH THAT FLUTTERS ROUND A LIGHT,
Risking my soul for love and love's delight:
In love with you I'm like the candle too,
Dissolving, burning, weeping, through the night.

🌱

زنهار بکوش تا توانی ای دل

ALWAYS, WHATEVER ELSE YOU DO, MY HEART,
Try to be kind, try to be true, my heart:
And if he's faithless, all may yet be well –
Who knows what he might do? Not you, my heart.

🌱

ای دل به جهانت ار بود راز و نیاز

MY HEART, IF YOU HAVE WORDS YOU NEED TO SAY,
Be warned! Keep would-be confidants away.
Seek help from no one here: five times a day
The entrance to His court stands open. Pray.

❦

از عمر عزیزم حاصلم چیست بگو

WHAT HAS THIS LIFE WE LONG FOR GIVEN ME? TELL ME.
Who looks on me with any sympathy? Tell me.
With all one's goods and chattels gone, without a home,
How long can one survive in penury? Tell me.

❦

اگر به بند زمانه کسی شود محبوس

WHEN SOMEONE IS IMPRISONED FOR A WHILE
Men ask about his fate, and want to know his crimes;
   If someone accidentally says my name,
Fear makes him beg to be excused, a thousand times.

❦

با ندیمان خوش و صحبت یاران لطیف

A PICNIC AT THE DESERT'S EDGE, WITH WITTY FRIENDS,
And tambourines, and harps, and lutes, is very sweet.
And if my lover, for a moment, should drop by,
I'll grill his liver with my body's fiery heat.

❦

Jahan Malek Khatun • 189

اى دل گل روى يار ديدن چه خوش است

TO SEE THE BLOSSOM OF HIS FACE, MY HEART — HOW SWEET;
To nibble kisses from his lips, my heart – how sweet;
To snatch a moment's happiness, exchanged for so much sorrow –
To gain my soul, and sacrifice my heart – how sweet.

🦋

تدبير و صواب از دل خوش بايد جست

A HAPPY HEART'S THE PLACE FOR PLANS AND PIETY,
And wealth's a fine foundation for sobriety:
A weak and wasted arm can't wield a warrior's sword,
A broken heart can't act with cold propriety.

🦋

تا بر درت ای دوست مرا باری نیست

IF I CAN'T EVEN GET BEYOND YOUR DOOR,
> that's hard for me –

What heart-felt heavy burden could weigh more?
> that's hard for me.

If you'll be kind and patient with me, that's
> not hard for me;

If, when you think of me, you're not so sure –
> that's hard for me.

🦋

بیچاره کسی که از وطن دور شود

PITY THE WRETCH, FORCED FROM HER NATIVE LAND,
With no one close, to hear or understand –
World-weary, heart-sick, unprovided for,
Alone, and at her enemies' command.

🦋

ازدل نالم یا ز فلک یا ز فراق

SHALL I COMPLAIN OF ABSENCE? OF MY HEART? OR OF THE SKIES?
Or that I lack the patient strength to suffer and be wise?
The heavens' harshness means my soul is ready to depart . . .
(That harshness, and my fawning friends' hypocrisy and lies).

❦

گل گفت به خنده صبحدم با بلبل

LAUGHING, THE ROSE SAID TO THE NIGHTINGALE ONE DAY,
"How long will you keep up this constant racket, pray?
I'm leaving here, I'll pack and I'll be on my way . . . "
Now don't you get ideas from what these roses say!

❦

ازتهمت خصم نیستم آسوده

MY ENEMIES' GLIB LIES ARE NEVER DONE –
How long will their cruel calumnies go on?
I'm like the wretched wolf (who'd done no harm)
Accused of killing Joseph, Jacob's son.

شیراز خوش است خاصه درفصل بهار

SHIRAZ WHEN SPRING IS HERE – WHAT PLEASURE EQUALS THIS?
With streams to sit by, wine to drink, and lips to kiss,
With mingled sounds of drums and lutes and harps and flutes;
Then, with a nice young lover near, Shiraz is bliss.

Obayd-e Zakani

In arts and sciences, don't try to be a master,
Unless you want to be, like me, a big disaster;
To catch the eye of princes, just suck up to them,
Sing silly songs, fuck boys — and you'll get on much faster.

قدم از خطهٔ شیراز و به جان در خطرم

I'VE SET OUT FROM SHIRAZ, I'VE PUT
                    my fearful soul in danger;
I have no choice, I bleed for grief,
                    I've made myself a stranger;

I wave my arms about, I'm soaked
                    in mud from head to toe,
And what's my profit from all this?
                    That's what I'd like to know!

I'm shrieking like a nightingale,
                    and then I'm like the rose
He wildly sings to as it's opening,
                    tearing off my clothes;

And if I quit my town it means
                    I'm done for; look, if I
Should even venture from my street,
                    I know I'm sure to die.

Don't ask about my journey, friends,
                    just think of me as gone,
Because I haven't got a clue
                    about what's going on.

Out of Shiraz, I'm hopeless, helpless,
           I just pine and fret;
Over my shoulder I look back,
           distracted by regret.

I haven't strength to hold my reins,
           and really there's no knowing
What these poor feet are up to,
           or where it is we're going.

I'm so fed up, my father's words,
           my friends' commiseration
Can't do a single thing today
           to help the situation.

But O Obayd, a trip like this
           is not the one for me –
It's Fate that drags me in its chains,
           my fate, my destiny!

قصهٔ درد دل و غصهٔ شب های دراز

MY HURT HEART'S TALES, MY NIGHTS' TRAVAILS, AH, WHERE
Can I recount the forms of my despair?

I've no companion now to sit with, no
Kind friend to hear the secrets I could share,

And I'm more wretched that my wretchedness
Finds no one who might hear me out or care.

But happiness's dawn must come, for all
The nights of misery I've had to bear.

The world ignores the indigent: O God,
Now men reject me, show me You're still there;

O Comforter of all the wretched, help
Obayd's unhappy heart, and heed his prayer.

نسیم باد مصلّی و آب رکن آباد

THE BREEZE OF MOSALLA, AND ROKNABAD'S
                              clear stream will take
The memory of a stranger's home away,
                    for this town's sake.

Joy to this heart-delighting place, joy, peace,
                         prosperity –
And may its excellence endure for all
                         eternity!

Turn where you will here, there are nightingales'
                         sweet trills and sighs,
In every meadow you pass by you'll see
                         tall box-trees rise.

Look where you will, and girls as lovely as
                         Shirin are there,
Go where you will, and lovers like Farhad
                         are everywhere.

My heart's in love with this bewitching town –
                         whose lovely site
Fills all my heart with happiness, my mind
                         with sheer delight.

My mind remembers my home-town, but I
                              cannot break free
Of this Shiraz's ringlets – her black locks
                              have captured me!

Help! Save me from her hyacinthine curls,
                              her heathen ways,
Her bold narcissus eyes, their magically
                              deceitful gaze!

But these are spoils, consider them as spoils –
                              take what you can;
Frail is our body and feeble, and brief
                              the life of man!

Grasp at her skirts now, do what you will, do all
                              you're able to;
Drink wine, and let the future come, since what
                              is that to you?

Choose wine then, and the flute, and hear the tale
                              both have to say –
"The world is built on water, like the wind
                              men pass away."

Pleasure's a blessing, and the world is sweet –
                              Obayd, though, chooses
To be the slave of one whose noble heart
                              all this refuses.

افتاده ایم تنها در کنج بی‌نوایی

HERE IN OUR CORNER, WRETCHED AND UNDONE,
Free of faith's comforts, quite content to shun

The world and patronage, uninterested
In anything that might be going on –

Here with our souls' companions, bored to death
With hypocrites and all they claim they've done,

No pompous pride disturbs our minds, no thoughts
Of purity – no, not a single one!

We've drunk the poison of our indigence
And don't want antidotes from anyone.

Happy the man who's friends with misery
And rules in poverty's domains; he's done

What wise Obayd has, who is not ashamed
That beggary's the kingdom he has won.

گر آن مه را وفا بودی چه بودی

IF THAT FULL MOON WERE TRUE AND GOOD,
                    how would that be?
And if he feared God as he should,
                    how would that be?

I'd like to stay with him a while –
If he decided that I could,
                    how would that be?

I long to kiss his lovely lips,
And if he said he thought I should,
                    how would that be?

And if that idol I pursue
Pursued me too, and understood,
                    how would that be?

Or if one day that king should glance
At where this helpless beggar stood,
                    how would that be?

If wisdom followed me around,
Or if I'd sense and hardihood,
                    how would that be?

If happiness should lead Obayd
To him, supposing that it could,
                    how would that be?

ای کیرگاه دیوی و گاهی فرشته

DEVIL, AND THEN ANGEL — IS IT THE SAME YOU?
Which are you then, my prick? How should I name you?
You and that cunt of hers — no man alive
Can hope to get away from you, or tame you;
There is no mind that doesn't dream of you,
In every house the seeds you've sown proclaim you.

خیزم سوی بازار گذاری بکنم

I'M OFF TO STROLL THROUGH THE BAZAAR — AND THERE
I'll see what can be flushed out from its lair;
I'll lure a rent-boy home here, or a whore;
One of the two — either will do — I don't care.

این کیر که از منار شده بالاتر

THIS TOOL OF MINE THAT'S TALLER THAN OUR MINARET
Is grander than our preacher's prick, and more thickset;
It gets progressively more young as I grow old,
It grows more stubborn-hard the flabbier I get.

🌿

زر نیست که قصد کون نازی بکنم

I'D LIKE A BOY TO FUCK — BUT I CAN'T PAY;
I'd like some wine to while away the day —
But as I've got no cash for carnal pleasures,
It seems there's nothing left to do but pray.

🌿

مرا قرض هست و دگر هیچ نیست

I'VE DEBTS, AND NOTHING ELSE: ENDLESS
    expenses, and no money:
"The world's all pleasure, so enjoy!"
    To me that isn't funny.
I'm talentless, or bad luck's made
    my talents disappear –
I've let the reins of life go slack,
    and now I'm sick with fear.
Time to get on your knees, Obayd,
    to see what God can do,
This endless begging door to door
    is not the life for you.

❧

دل در پی وصل دلبران است هنوز

MY HEART STILL HANKERS AFTER HER,
My past life haunts me still, as strong as ever;
  We said, "Together we'll grow old"
And I've grown old, and she's still young as ever.

❧

قومی زپی مذهب و دین می سوزند

SOME ARE ON FIRE FOR FAITH'S SAKE, SOME TO SEE
The houris promised for eternity.
My garden, wine, and lover are like heaven:
The faithful burn – in fires of jealousy!

❧

بعد از چهلت نشاط هستی نبود

AFTER FORTY YOUR SPRIGHTLY DAYS ARE DONE,
After fifty your weaknesses have won,
After sixty don't hope for happiness,
And after seventy your health has gone.

❧

کوعشرت شیراز و می اندہ سوز

WHERE IS SHIRAZ'S WINE, THAT BURNED OUR GRIEF AWAY?
And those brisk, pretty boys who served us, where are they?
Tomorrow if, in heaven, there is no wine or pleasure,
God's heaven will be hell, just like Shiraz today.

دی کردکش تواضعی با کیرم

HER PUSSY HAD THE KINDNESS TO INVITE
My prick to stay and dine with her last night;
Damn him, he didn't even rise to greet her . . .
It's shameful that my prick's so impolite!

ای آنکه بجز تو نیست فریادرسی

O GOD, SOLE HELP OF MEN IN MISERY,
Let mercy temper Your authority:
Please fix my wretchedness, since this would mean
Nothing to You, but quite a lot to me!

🌸

جانا تو را هنوز بدین حسن و این جمال

MY PRETTY DEAR, YOU'RE STILL TOO YOUNG TO MAKE
The pilgrimage to Mecca and repent,

But if you feel the need to be a pilgrim,
Take my advice, my dear, it's kindly meant:

Straddle my prick and ride it – that can be
Your thousand-pilgrimage equivalent.

🌸

کس گفت که کیر را خوش انگیختهاند

PUSSY REMARKED, "THIS PRICK'S A MASTERPIECE,
They've hung the balls beneath it very nicely;
From tip to toe, you'd say that it's as though
They'd followed my prerequisites precisely."

۔۔

در عمر خود این طبیبک هرزه مقال

THIS NONSENSE-SPOUTING DOCTOR COULDN'T SEE
A patient and not kill him instantly:
Last night Death came to him and said, "For once
You'll buy what you've been selling, and from me."

۔۔

برخیزم و چارهٔ خماری بکنم

I'LL FIX THIS HANGOVER, THEN FIND A WHORE
Who'll be prepared to let me through her door;
And then my prick will either have her cunt
Or ass, but which of them I'm not quite sure.

🌿

کیرم که در این تموز شد تاب زده

IT'S SUMMER, AND MY PRICK'S TOO HOT TODAY,
It's stiff with wine and eager for the fray;
I'll take it down to pussy's shady bower –
That's cool and moist, the perfect place to stay.

🌿

این کیر که سرو جویبار کس توست

MY PRICK'S A CYPRESS THAT GROWS TALL AND STRAIGHT
Beside your pussy's stream, as is appropriate;
But come here quickly as it's getting late
For him to stand around alone like this and wait.

❦

آمد رمضان و موسم باده برفت

RAMADAN'S COME — THE TIME FOR PASSING WINE AROUND
has gone;
The season when we bragged and drank and laughed and clowned
has gone;
All of the wine that we've been hoarding still remains
undrunk,
And, still unfucked, the gaggle of cheap whores we found
has gone.

❦

هر چند که کون لطف و صفایی دارد

ALTHOUGH THE ASS CAN BE ENTICING AND ATTRACTIVE
It's drawn too tight, the air there's pretty putrefactive –
No, take the cunt, it's nicely moist, and grassy too,
And anyway there's much more room there to be active.

کس ِ بکری به دست شخصی افتاد

AN INDIVIDUAL FUCKED WITH ALL HIS MIGHT
A virgin cunt, still girlish, small, and tight;
The cunt said to the prick, "How nice it is
When hopes come true, and everything's just right!"

پیش از این از ملک هر سالی

WELL, ONCE UPON A TIME, IN DRIBS AND DRABS,
Income turned up for me, throughout the year;

I'd dry bread and fresh herbs to hand, in case
A friend should unexpectedly appear;

And sometimes there'd be wine to drink, for when
A pretty boy or sweet young girl came here.

But now I'm getting on in years, my life
Has suddenly become much more austere;

I've neither dry to eat, nor wet to drink,
And all that's in my house is me, my dear.

❦

می‌کوش که تا زامل نظر خواندت

TRY HARD TO HAVE MEN MAKE A FUSS OF YOU
And say, "He knows what's right, he sees what's true."
Then if you're good they'll say, "Oh, he's an angel";
And if you're wicked, "There, he's human too!"

❦

Obayd-e Zakani • 213

The Lesson to be Learned from the End of
King Sheikh Abu Es'haq

ABU ES'HAQ, WORLD'S LORD, AT WHOSE COMMAND
Crowns were distributed throughout this land,
Tales of whose glorious generosity
Enthralled the world with his nobility –
Qobad and Afrasyab shared his domain,
An Ardavan, a Sanjar, in his reign,
Surpassing faith with wisdom, one whose arm
Revived the world, protecting it from harm,
A Khosrow in the pleasures of his days,
A King Anushirvan of righteous ways,
Who built fine porticoes, a splendid fort
In which a king could fittingly hold court,
And gardens of a heavenly design
Where he would take his ease and drink his wine;
Whose slaves, admitted to this court, became
Like noblemen and kings in all but name.

Look at the game Fate played, and how Disaster
Tugged at his court's reins, and is now its master;
Catastrophe has swept away his son,
His government, and kingdom – all are gone!
And that great garden whose magnificence
Once rivaled paradise's elegance,
That haunt of nightingales . . . lies stripped and bare –
A harsh, black-hearted crow has nested there;

That glorious fortress with its splendid riches
Is home to owls now, and to whelping bitches.
Obayd, from this sad downfall we can learn
A thousand clues to how the heavens turn;
Pity the wretch who grasps at stars, who tries
To hold on to the turning of the skies;
Lucky the man whose heart's content, who stays
Indifferent to the world's inconstant ways.

موش و گربه

Cat and Mouse

Possessed of wisdom, common sense or learning,
I guarantee that it'll knock you flat –
This story's of a mouse, and of a cat.

O wise and knowledgeable one, rehearse
This Cat and Mouse tale in well-ordered verse,
Like pearls that roll from rhyme to chiming rhyme.
In old Kerman then, once upon a time,
There lived a lion-tailed cat – huge, dragon-jawed,
Pot-bellied, barrel-chested, leopard-clawed.
He'd miaow – and roaring lions would leave their feast,
Fleeing in terror from the savage beast.
He dropped by at his favorite bar one day
To hunt for mice – and waiting for his prey
(Just like a thief behind a rock), our cat
Prepared his ambush, prone behind a vat.

Then suddenly a little mouse peered out,
Saw the coast clear and gave his squeaky shout,
Dashed for the vat and let his mouse head sink
Deep in the dark intoxicating drink.
Now roaring drunk he cried, "Where is that cat?
I'll cut his head off and I'll flay the brat,

I'll stuff his skin with straw; that cat to me's
The most contemptible of enemies."
The cat sat listening and he hardly breathed;
Slowly his teeth were bared, his claws unsheathed,
And then he pounced and like a leopard pinned
The mouse who squirmed and squealed, "I know I've
   sinned,
I'm sorry, I . . . " The cat replied, "I heard –
You hypocrite, you Moslem – every word,
You can't fool me." And there and then he killed
The mouse and ate it. With his belly filled
He strolled off to the mosque, and glibly said
His prayers as if a mullah born and bred:
"Court of the Highest, I repent; no more
Will my sharp teeth be soaked in mouse's gore –
And for the blood that I've unjustly shed
I'll give the poor as alms twelve rounds of bread."
He prayed and moaned and heaved such bitter sighs
That tears stood brimming in his feline eyes.
Behind the pulpit lurked a little mouse
Who quickly bore the news off to his house:
"Great news, the cat's converted, he repents,
He's filled with sacred Moslem sentiments;
This paragon of pious virtues keeps
Prayer vigils in the mosque, and moans and weeps."

Then when they heard the news the laughing mice
Seemed blessed with all the joys of paradise,
And seven elders of the mousey nation
Were chosen as a special deputation –

Each of them carried something rare and fine
To give the cat: one bore a glass of wine
And one a spit of lamb kebab; another
Took currants in a salver, while his brother
Sported a tray of figs; one cheese he'd made,
And one a syrup of sweet lemonade;
One bore him yogurt, butter, and fresh bread,
The last a tray of rice upon his head.
The mice drew near the cat – and with salaams
And deepest bows and eulogistic psalms
They greeted him: "O thou, for whom all mice
Would undergo the final sacrifice,
Accept the gifts we offer you, O lord."

He peered at them, and chanted, "Your reward
Will be in heaven; I've fasted now for days
To please the Merciful beyond all praise;
Whoever does God's work it's certain he
Will be rewarded, and abundantly!"
Then he continued: "But come closer, do . . .
Dear friends, a few steps more, a very few . . . "
Then, frail as trembling aspen leaves, the mice
Went forward as a group – and in a trice
The cat leapt like a mighty champion, like
A fighter who sees when and where to strike;
Five mice he captured – two in each front paw
And one was snapped up in his lion-like jaw.

The two remaining mice that got away
Fled crying, "Slothful mice, oh rue the day –

With claws and teeth the cat's dismembered five
Of us and only we remain alive."
Then at this bitter news the grieving crowd
Donned mourning clothes, lamented long and loud,
Heaped dust upon their heads and, contrite, cried,
"Alas for our great leaders who have died!"
At last the mice were able to agree,
"We'll tell the king of this calamity;
Before the throne we'll chronicle our case –
The foul oppression of the feline race."

The mouse king sat upon his throne in state;
Far off he saw his subjects congregate
Until they came before him as a crowd
And, with a single motion, deeply bowed:
"O king of kings and of the ages king,
This cat has done a hideous, dreadful thing;
O king of kings, we are your sacrifice,
An annual one of us would once suffice
To feed this cat; but, since his late conversion,
Since he's become a pious Moslem Persian,
Five at a time is now his greedy style."
And when they'd whimpered and complained a while,
The king replied: "My dearest subjects, wait!
I'll be revenged upon this reprobate,
I'll kill this cat in such a way the story
Will fill the world with my eternal glory."
He spent a whole week mustering his men,
Three hundred thousand mice-at-arms, and then
Another thirty thousand; each mouse bore
A bow and spear and shield, and longed for war;

Now like a wave they poured in from Gilan,
From distant Rasht and fertile Khorasan.
The brave victorious mouse addressed the horde:
"I speak now as your leader and your lord,
A mouse must be our envoy to this cat;
Our message is, 'Submit, or failing that
You must prepare yourself for endless war.'
There was an ancient mouse ambassador
Who was entrusted with the valiant plan;
He traveled to the cat's lair in Kerman
And there he bowed and said, "I represent
The noble mouse king and his government,
And bear a message meant for you alone:
You must pay homage to the mouse king's throne;
War is the price if you do not submit!"
The cat replied, "I never heard such shit!
I'll not budge from Kerman!" But secretly
He summoned cats to his confederacy,
Cats like lions, cats from Isfahan,
Wild cats from Yazd, cats from his own Kerman;
And when their army'd grown they set out for
The destined conflict, well prepared for war.

Across the desert marched the mousey horde,
Down from the hills the feline army poured,
The plain of Pars became their battlefield –
Each side fought bravely and refused to yield.
(So great the slaughter was no man could say
How many cats and mice were killed that day.)

The cat sprang like a lion, and attacked
The center where the mice were thickly packed –
But one mouse trailed his horse, the cat spun round
And as he spun fell headlong to the ground;
"Allah is with us!" cried the mice. "We've won –
Grab him, grab the cats' doughty champion!"
They beat their war-drums wildly to proclaim
That victory was theirs, and martial fame;
The troops milled round, excited, jubilant,
Mobbing their mouse king on his elephant.
The cat's front paws were tied and tightly bound,
They forced him as a suppliant to the ground;
The king's command rang out, "String up that cat,
Hang the abominable black-faced brat."

But hearing this, his feline pride provoked,
The cat seethed like a cauldron, panted, choked . . .
Then like a lion he knelt and gnawed to shreds
His captors' bonds; they snapped like flimsy threads.
He grabbed the nearest mice and glared around
Then flung them with contempt against the ground –
The mice fled squeaking in a mass defection,
Their king fled in the opposite direction:
The elephant, his royal rider too,
His wealth and crown and splendid retinue,
Decamped and disappeared; on that wide plain
Not one of them was ever seen again.
And all that's left is this peculiar story
Bestowing posthumous, poetic glory
On old Obayd-e Zakani.

My son,
Consider carefully who lost, who won:
Store up this story's useful implications,
Remember it in tricky situations.

Explanatory Notes

The reader is referred to the Introduction for a more detailed treatment of the historical background to the poems, such as the rulers of Shiraz, their families, and their rivalries. The poetic conventions of the period – for example, the treatment of gender, the question as to whether poems are to be considered as primarily secular or mystical – are also discussed more fully in the Introduction.

HAFEZ

pp. 2–3, However old, incapable

ancient Zoroastrian . . . entered in his court: The predominant pre-Islamic religion of Iran had been Zoroastrianism, and the faith retained a strong presence in Iran for a number of centuries after the Islamic conquest, although by Hafez's time the number of Zoroastrians still living in the country had greatly diminished (many had emigrated to India, where they formed the Parsi community). In medieval Iran, Zoroastrianism survived as a local, non-Islamic indigenous religious tradition; many scholars believe that it had a profound influence on the growth of Iranian Islamic mysticism, particularly through the writings of the twelfth-century illuminationist philosopher Sohravardi, whose teachings combine Islamic, neo-Platonist, and Zoroastrian elements. In Hafez's poems "Zoroastrian" (or "Magian," the words have the same meaning) is usually shorthand for a way of looking at or experiencing the world that does not conform to the expectations and requirements of orthodox Islam.

"Ancient Zoroastrian" here translates a phrase, rendered elsewhere in this book as "Magian sage," that is common in Hafez's poetry and which has been given two almost diametrically opposed interpretations. The "mystical" interpretation takes the old Zoroastrian to mean a Sufi sheikh, or someone who passes on religious or mystical insights outside of an orthodox Islamic context. Virtually every time this old Zoroastrian appears in Hafez's verses, wine is also mentioned soon afterwards (as in this poem), and in this mystical interpretation "wine" indicates an insight or knowledge imparted by the sheikh, one that produces the "intoxication" of mystical experience. In support of this interpretation it is pointed out that the word in the phrase for "old"/"ancient" (*pir*) is also a designation for a Sufi sheikh; however, *pir* can also mean simply "old man," without any implications of particular sagacity or mystical expertise. A more literal interpretation of the phrase takes the old Zoroastrian as the keeper of a wine-shop/tavern (as Moslems were forbidden to make or sell wine, these activities were carried out by members of the religious minorities, including Jews and Christians as well as Zoroastrians), and the wine that he sells as actual wine. My own feeling, shared by many but probably still a minority of Hafez's readers, is that the poet, usually and primarily, intends the literal meaning, although a suggestion of the "mystical" meaning is often there as well. In this more literal interpretation, the Zoroastrian's "court" would be his wine-shop/tavern.

pp. 6–7, I see no love in anyone

Khezr: a figure in the Qur'an who is a contemporary
of Moses. His name means "the green man." In the
Islamic versions of the Alexander romance (a romanticized
biography of Alexander the Great, found in both the
Christian and Islamic medieval worlds), he is the keeper
of the waters of eternal life, and Hafez's line alludes to
this; for Sufis he represents someone who receives direct
illumination from God.

The ball of generosity . . . No rider comes to strike it:
The metaphor is from polo, which was very popular in
medieval Persian courts, and is often mentioned in poetry
of the period.

p. 8, The orchard charms our hearts, and chatter when

*Sing, nightingale! Rosebuds unopened yet . . . your fear – is
sweet:* The nightingale's love for the rose, as a metaphor
for hopeless human love-longing, is a common trope
in medieval Persian poetry. Often the nightingale also
represents the poet who speaks the poem. In this poem
the nightingale's fear is of the roses' departure, when their
petals fall, which the nightingale anxiously foresees even
before the rosebuds have begun to open. This anxiety
produces the nightingale's song, which is sweet both to
the listener and to the nightingale, in the sense that love is
bitter-sweet ("your fear – is sweet").

pp. 10–11, Come, boy, and pass the wine around

Come, boy, and pass the wine around: It was not uncommon for a poet to incorporate a line or half-line by another poet into a poem, as a compliment to the poet in question. The first half-line of this poem (i.e. the first line of the translation) is in Arabic, and used to be traditionally ascribed to the early Omayyad caliph Yazid ibn Mo'awiyeh. The borrowing by Hafez from such a source was thought to be scandalous since Yazid is one of the most hated of the Omayyads, particularly by the Shi'a, as he was responsible for the murder of Hossein, the son of the caliph Ali, who is especially revered in Shi'ism. Even more scandalous was the fact that this is the first poem in Hafez's Divan, so that Hafez appeared to be opening his collection of poems with something close to blasphemy. Various later poets commented on the borrowing, one saying that it was "A great fault for a lion to snatch a morsel from the mouth of a dog," and another defending Hafez, recalling how the latter had appeared to him in a dream and said, "It is licit for a believer to take the goods of a heretic." But the literary scholar Mohammad Qazvini (1874–1949) established that the half-line was not in fact by Yazid at all, and the puzzle as to why Hafez should apparently borrow from (and by implication compliment) such a hated figure was resolved.

And if the wine-seller says wine: See the note to pp. 2–3

pp. 12–13, No one has seen your face, and yet

the Sufi meeting house / And wine-shop are one place: See the note to pp. 2–3.

p. 14, To tell you now my poor heart's state

And in the darkness of the night, to pierce the pearl / That is so fine and delicate: to a Western reader the obvious meaning here is sexual, and this implication is certainly there in Hafez's Persian. But piercing a pearl is a metaphor for a number of things in Persian poetry; one meaning is to speak charmingly (and by extension to write fine poetry), and this is implied by Hafez's line – piercing the pearl is indulging in the sweet nothings of lovers' conversation; another meaning, sometimes present in Sufi verse, is to arrive at the essence of something valuable or longed-for, and this meaning is also present here – to know the sweet essence of love. These implications are at least as important as the sexual meaning in the Persian.

p. 15, Thanks be to God now that the wine-shop door

Majnun's grief, Layla's curls, Ayaz's foot . . . Mahmud's face: Majnun and Layla, and Mahmud and Ayaz, are lovers celebrated in Persian poetry. The love between Majnun and Layla was fictional (the story is of Arab origin, but was well known in Persian culture; in Arabic the lovers' names mean Maddened and Night), heterosexual, and unsuccessful/unconsummated. That between Mahmud and Ayaz was historical (Mahmud was the Turkic Ghaznavid king, Mahmud of Ghazni, who ruled from 997 to 1030; Ayaz was a slave whom he loved and whom he made commander of his armies), homosexual, and successful/consummated. So by choosing these two pairs of lovers as representative, Hafez is covering a good number of the possibilities of how love might be.

Your eyebrow's curve: In a mosque a niche in the wall, called the *mehrab*, shows the direction of Mecca, towards which the worshippers pray. The beloved's eyebrow is implicitly compared to the curve at the top of the *mehrab*, indicating that the speaker of the poem directs his prayers not toward Mecca but to the belovèd. The trope is common in medieval Persian poetry, as is the comparison of the beloved's eyebrow to other beautiful curved objects, such as the new moon (see the final two lines on p. 150)

p. 16, Wine in my glass, and roses in my arms

I'll haunt these ruins . . . treasure of my love: Ruins were quite common in the medieval Persian landscape, for a number of reasons: Iran is a major earthquake zone, and for around two thousand years cities and palaces had been erected there; domestic buildings tended to be made of clay bricks, and these fell into ruin fairly easily; the wars of the thirteenth and fourteenth centuries had resulted in the partial or complete destruction of many once flourishing towns and villages.

The association of ruins and treasure is an old one in Persian poetry. Legend had it that ruins might be the site of hidden treasure (and perhaps sometimes they were). In this poem the speaker's heart is ruined by his longing, and the treasure his heart hides is his love for the poem's addressee. "Ruins" were also a place for the disreputable to gather and drink (with a suggestion that they too were "ruined"), and for this reason "ruins" became a slang word for a wine-shop, a place to drink and forget one's sorrows; this meaning too is hovering around the image.

the morals officer: the contemptuous name given by the Shirazis to their conqueror Mobarez al-din, who closed the wine-shops, forbade music, and was generally a royal pain in the neck.

Ramadan: the Moslem month of fasting and abstinence from sensual pleasure.

pp. 18–19 Go, mind your own business, preacher! What's all

eight heavens: Medieval cosmology was essentially Ptolemaic, with the earth at the center of the universe and surrounded by eight heavens nesting within one another.

My being's built upon those ruins: See the note to p. 16.

pp. 20–21, Welcome sweet flower, no one's

sheikh: a religious leader, assumed to be severe in his habits and to abstain from wine drinking.

Sultan Ovays: a Jalayerid prince who ruled in Baghdad from 1356 to 1374. He was an enemy of Mobarez al-din, the conqueror of Shiraz who was hated by Hafez. It's likely that, during the reign of Mobarez, Hafez sought patronage outside of Shiraz, and Sultan Ovays, as the enemy of a ruler he despised, would be a natural choice for him to offer his services to.

pp. 22–23 Come, so that we can scatter flowers

Kosar's stream: a stream in paradise, mentioned in the Qur'an.

pp. 24–25 A corner of the wine-shop is

Zoroastrians: See the note to pp. 2–3.

p. 28, Those days when loving friends would meet

Zendehrud: the river that runs through Isfahan.

Karan's pastoral retreat: Karan was a garden near Isfahan, bordering the river Zendehrud.

p. 29, Lost Joseph will return to Canaan's land again

Joseph … His grieving father's house: The story of Joseph being sold into slavery by his brothers, and then rising to the highest honors in Egypt, appears in the biblical Book of Genesis, and in the Qur'an. The Qur'anic version of the tale is greatly admired in the Islamic world, and is referred to as "the best of stories." The grief of Joseph's father, Jacob, at the loss of his son is a frequent trope in medieval Persian poetry.

p. 32, What's all this hiding happiness and wine away?

Jamshid's skull, and King Qobad's … Kay Kavus, or Bahman: These four figures are all legendary pre-Islamic Persian kings.

Farhad's blood-red tears: Farhad was a stone-mason who fell in love with the princess Shirin, who was married to King Khosrow Parviz (a historical king of Sasanid Iran, who ruled from 590 to 628). Farhad's love was unrequited and he committed suicide.

tulips … like a wine-glass: Small, red, wild tulips are meant. Their shape resembles a wine-glass's and their red color is like the wine visible through the glass.

Unless these ruins hold a treasure: See the note to p. 16.

Mosalla's breeze, and Roknabad's clear stream: Mosalla is a garden near Shiraz (Hafez's tomb is there); Roknabad is the name given to a stream and its surrounding area near Shiraz.

p. 33, I've known the pains of love's frustration — ah, don't ask!

You bite your lip at me: that is, in reproach.

pp. 34–35 That you're a pious prig by nature

My father let his chance of heaven's grace: Tempting though it is to think that this might refer to Hafez's own father, the commentators agree that it refers to Adam as the father of mankind.

pp. 36–37, I saw the green fields of the sky

go, climb / Like Jesus through the skies: In Islamic belief, Jesus was not crucified, and did not die, but was rapt straight into heaven by God; the line's implication is that Hafez too will be taken straight to heaven.

Don't trust the shining moon: A literal translation would be "star of night," which suggests the evening star to us, but the commentators agree that the rising moon is meant. The moon is an emblem of both mutability and fate, which together take away earthly sovereignty and glory.

Kay Kavus's throne ... the belt of Khosrow: Kay Kavus and Khosrow are legendary pre-Islamic kings. A particular kind of belt could indicate royalty or nobility (as it could in medieval Europe, too — hence the phrase "belted earl" which turns up occasionally in Victorian literature).

A pawn to make the sun and moon / precipitously yield: An example of the metaphorical use of chess, which is relatively common in the poetry of the period (see also the note to pp. 140–41).

The harvest of the moon's a grain, / and of the stars but two: The lines imply that all the love in the heavens is less than the love concentrated in "you." Hafez quite often suggests that heavenly love is a lesser thing than human love (although it is of course possible to take the "you" as referring to a manifestation of the divine). The line contains a lovely untranslatable pun, as the word for "harvest" also means "halo around the moon."

this Sufi cloak: Virtually every time Hafez mentions Sufis and Sufism, he does so in order to reject them. He quite often refers to himself, as here, as having been a Sufi, but then as thinking better of it.

pp. 38–39, What's sweeter than a garden and good talk

Garden of Eram: a legendary pre-Islamic garden said to be of great beauty.

Kosar's stream: see note to pp. 22–23.

p. 40, Last night I saw the angels

the seventy-two competing factions: There was a *hadith* (saying of the prophet Mohammad) that Islam would split into seventy-two (or seventy-three) sects.

pp. 42–43, For years my heart inquired of me

This is one of the most famous and extensively commented upon of Hafez's poems. It invokes, or at least alludes to, four religions: the "Magian sage" refers to Zoroastrianism, either literally or as a metaphor (see also the note to pp. 2–3); Moses and Jesus represent Judaism and Christianity respectively, and both figures are of course revered by Islam. The poem also invokes religious heterodoxy in the person of "That friend they hanged"; this refers to Hallaj, a Sufi martyred in the eighth century for saying, among other things, "I am the truth." Jamshid is a pre-Islamic Persian king; in his cup the secrets of the world could be seen (Hafez implies that it was a wine-cup, either literally or in the mystical sense of a means of insight into hidden truths). Sameri means "the Samaritan" and refers to the person who led the Israelites astray with the golden calf when Moses ascended Sinai. In its mixture of various religious groupings, and its mingling of references to both secular pleasures (the wine, the "beauties" of the poem's close) and mystical insight (Jamshid's cup, Hallaj's martyrdom), and in its recommendation that one look inward for the truth (the pearl the speaker thinks he has lost but in fact possesses), the poem is a concentrated example of Hafez's most polyphonic poetic strategies.

p. 45 When my love lifts his glass

This is a good example of how even an apparently very simple poem can be read in either a secular or mystical way, with the subject of the poem being either a young man or God. Until the last line, the poem reads as a secular love lyric, but the word translated as "divine" (which refers to the covenant made between man and God at the beginning of time) retroactively rewrites the poem as being about the love of God. This shift in apparent meaning is especially effective because the penultimate stanza, about the police, seems to anchor the poem so firmly in the mundane physical world. But, even with the addition of "divine," the poem can still be read as being about the speaker's love for a young man, with the further twist that this love was agreed on at the covenant, so that the poem once again becomes about secular love, but this time with a divine sanction. Or "divine" can be taken simply as a hyperbolic metaphor that means "my love is wonderful and will last for ever." The ambiguity is deliberate, and the poem is meant to be read as having equivocally secular or mystical meanings. To insist in a reductive fashion on only one of the possibilities is to set aside Hafez's multiple implications, and to diminish the poem.

When my love . . . comes tumbling down: The conceit in the first lines is that when the beloved appears, all other desirable people are disregarded, so that their "market" collapses. The trope is common in the poetry of the period.

pp. 46–47, Plant friendship's tree – the heart's desire

Majnun: the archetypal lover – see the note to p. 15.

pp. 48–49, To give up wine, and human beauty? And to give up love?

Magian sage: See the note to pp. 2–3.

sheikh: See the note to pp. 20–22

p. 50, That busybody criticizes me

Sohayb: a figure from the early years of Islam, proverbial for his asceticism.

pp. 54–55, At dawn, upon the breeze, I caught

Moslem beads: prayer beads, like a rosary.

his eyebrow's curve: See the note to p. 15.

pp. 56–57, Do you know what our harps and lutes advise us

the old Magian priest: a wine-seller – see note to pp. 2–3.

Qur'an reciters: The poet here puns on his own pen-name, "Hafez," which means, among other things, a Qur'an reciter. He refers to his religious namesakes with contempt, saying they are among those who "live by lies"; the musical instruments at the opening of the poem suggest the other meaning of "Hafez," a musician.

sheikhs: See the note to pp. 20–22

pp. 58–59: What memories! I once lived on

And to my eyes . . . your doorway shone: This sentence can also mean: "The brightness of my eyes was from the dust before your door," suggesting the dust was used as kohl, or eye-shadow.

Bu Es'haq: Abu Es'haq was the king deposed and killed by Mobarez al-din; he had been Hafez's most generous and faithful patron, and the poem is a lament for his death.

pp. 60–61, Though wine is pleasurable, and though the breeze

    morals officer: See the note to p. 16.

    Khosrow's crown . . . King Kasra's skull: One of Hafez's most direct attacks on Mobarez al-din and his laws against wine and music. Khosrow and Kasra are pre-Islamic kings, here probably used to evoke the kings against whom Mobarez al-din had fought – Abu Es'haq, and his older brother, Jalal al-din Masud Shah (the father of Jahan Malek Khatun); Obayd associates the same two pre-Islamic monarchs with the Inju kings in his lament for Abu Es'haq "The Lesson to be Learned from End of King Sheikh Abu Es'haq" (see the note to pp. 214–15).

    Pars . . . Baghdad: Pars (now called Fars) is the province of which Shiraz is the capital; Eraq is western Iran; Tabriz is the main town in Azerbaijan in the north west of the country; Baghdad was where Sultan Ovays ruled, and it was to him that Hafez appears to have turned for patronage while Mobarez al-din was ruling Shiraz.

pp. 62–3, May your dear body never need

    This poem seems to be addressed to a young prince or powerful aristocrat, and is best read as an elegant bid for patronage.

    And when the wind of autumn blows: The "wind of autumn" is a periphrasis for death, so that the line is saying, "May death pass you by, and leave you unharmed."

    evil eye . . . rue within your beauty's flames: Rue is still burned in Persian culture to ward off the evil eye.

pp. 66–7, You've sent no word of how you are

ancient wine-seller: See the note to pp. 2–3.

p. 68, Not every Sufi's trustworthy, or pure in spirit

Hafez's cloak: See the note to pp. 36–7.

p. 69, Good news, my heart! The breath of Christ is wafting here

Like "For years my heart inquired of me" (pp. 42–3), this poem invokes Christianity (the "breath of Christ"), Judaism (Moses), and Zoroastrianism (the "fire" of the third stanza), as well as Islam.

pp. 70–71, My love has sent no letter for

one sinuous line / To lure and capture me: There is a pun in the Persian; the word translated as "line" means both a line of handwriting and the thread of a snare to catch birds or small game.

pp. 72–3, Good wine, that doesn't stupefy

These "pilgrims": Almost certainly Sufis are meant.

pp. 74–5, The One who gave your lovely face its rosy

Farhad . . . Shirin: See the note to p. 32.

Qavam al-din: a governor of Kerman, in south-eastern Iran, and later the vizier of Shah Shoja, the son of Mobarez al-din. Qavam al-din was greatly esteemed by Hafez, who has a number of poems that mention him, and he was one of the poet's patrons. Shah Shoja turned against Qavam and had him executed.

The poem begins apparently as a love lyric, but towards the end reveals itself as a lament for Qavam, and an impotent cry for "Justice" as Hafez clearly saw Qavam's execution as unjust. This "swerve" in meaning and emotional direction is not unusual in medieval Persian lyric poetry (an Iranian friend once referred to it to me as "in the Persian DNA"), but Hafez tends to indulge in it more extensively and unexpectedly than most of his predecessors and contemporaries.

pp. 76–7, May I remember always when

This poem may be in memory of Hafez's patron, Abu Es'haq, or it may be one of a number of poems by Hafez that imply he had once been very close to a young prince who is now neglecting him. The verse suggests both an erotic relationship and a prince-courtier one, and the two were often written of in terms of each other, so that it is sometimes difficult to decide which is the primary meaning; this ambiguity is certainly deliberate. The end of the poem implies that the friend/prince had taken a hand in revising and correcting Hafez's poems.

Canopy: literally "parasol," as used to shade a Middle Eastern prince, but the Bois de Boulogne connotations of "parasol" were too insistent, so I settled on "canopy."

pp. 78–9, These preachers who make such a show

My master reigns among the ruins: The master is the wine-seller; the ruins are literal ruins or a tavern. See the note to p. 16.

The house / Where Magians meet: This is the wine-shop, while the "liquid that revives men's hearts" is wine; the mystical interpretation is that the house is a Sufi meeting place, and the liquid that revives men's hearts is the doctrines and practices of the Sufis. See also the note to pp. 2–3.

pp. 80–81, The nightingales are drunk, wine-red roses appear

men knew this and said, "Yes": This refers to the pact made at creation when God asks mankind, "Am I not your lord?" and mankind answers, "Yes." Hafez elaborates this as an assent to all the happiness and grief that living in the world entails.

Asef: the chief minister of King Solomon. Riding the wind and understanding the language of the birds were said to be among Solomon's accomplishments.

pp. 84–85, Perhaps, my heart, the wine-shops' doors

One of a number of poems by Hafez referring to the closing of the wine-shops by Mobarez al-din, who is the "ascetic" referred to in the second stanza. Grape's fair child is wine, which has been "murdered" (i.e., banished). The metaphor is an elaboration of a long tradition in Persian poetry of the "murder" of the grape in order to make wine. "Grape's fair child" and "daughter of the vine" (see the first line on p. 109) are both quite common periphrases for wine in Persian poetry. As in a number of poems, Hafez ends by saying he may wear a Sufi cloak at times but underneath he's not "really" a Sufi at all.

pp. 86–7, *We haven't travelled to this door*

Hafez, cast off this Sufi cloak: See the note to pp. 84–5.

pp. 90–91, *Dear friends, that friend with whom we once*

Like "May I remember always when" (pp. 76-7), this poem seems to refer to Hafez's past relationship with a prince or powerful nobleman, who has now apparently forgotten him. The "friend" mentioned in the first line, and implicitly invoked throughout the poem, is probably Hafez himself.

pp. 92–3 *It is the night of power*

the night of power: This phrase refers to the night on which the first revelation of the Qur'an was made to the prophet Mohammad, by the angel Gabriel. Typically, Hafez suggests both religious and erotic meanings as the poem goes forward.

pp. 96–7, *Of all the roses in the world*

The monastery / Where Magians live: Magians – Zoroastrians – did not have monasteries, so this cannot be meant literally. Given the association of "Magians" with wine, which is everywhere in Hafez's poetry (see the note to pp. 2–3), the primary intended meaning is almost certainly a wine-shop/ tavern. The mystical interpretation would be that this itself is a metaphor, for a Sufi meeting place.

See how the world's bazaar pays cash: in distinction to religion's "payment" of heaven, which is in the nature of a promissory note.

pp. 98–9, A loving friend, good wine, a place secure

My tears are ruby-red: Tears are often referred to as red in Persian poetry; the conceit is that it is blood that is wept. This motif turns up occasionally in European medieval poetry too (for example in Chaucer's *Troilus and Criseyde*).

Towards the end of the poem Hafez's rhetoric becomes quite over the top, and the addressee responds in the final stanza with a remark that means, "Very seductive phrases, but you needn't think I'm so stupid as to be taken in."

pp. 100–101, Last night the wine-seller, a man

Venus dance in heaven: See the note to pp. 118–19.

Sorush: a pre-Islamic, Zoroastrian angel, who continued to be invoked in Persian poetry after Iran became a predominantly Moslem country. In the Moslem period he is often seen as giving those to whom he speaks insight into hidden truths.

And if your heart is red with blood: "Blood" here means "suffering," so an equivalent would be: "And if you're heart-broken."

Asef: used generically for a powerful lord, particularly a king's vizier or chief minister. See the note to pp. 80–81.

pp. 102–3, Love's road's an endless road

   the new moon's sliver: The new moon at the end of
Ramadan, the month of fasting, is eagerly watched for, as it
means the time of austerity is over.

pp. 104–5, My heart, good fortune is the only friend

   our ancient Zoroastrian: See the note to pp. 2–3. His
"precincts" are the wine-shop. The prayers mentioned
toward the end of the poem can be taken as literal prayers,
particularly if one reads the wine-shop and the wine
mystically, but in a more secular interpretation they could
also refer to wine drunk (or to love making) at night and
then first thing in the morning (the morning draught of
wine to clear one's head, on the "hair of the dog" principle,
is a commonplace of medieval Persian poetry).

pp. 106–7, Although our preacher might not like

   he's such a hypocrite: Hypocrisy is the unpardonable sin
for Hafez, and he is the first significant medieval Persian
poet to make his contempt for it such a prominent feature
of his poetry.

pp. 108–9, When you drink wine, sprinkle

   six directions: the geometrical directions an architect
would use: right, left, up, down, forward, and backward.

   daughter of the vine: See the note to pp. 84–5.

pp. 110–11, My heart was stolen by a lout

   Sufi cloaks: See the note to pp. 36–7.

An angel has no notion . . . pour on Adam's dust: The meaning is that love belongs to the human, not the angelic, world; angels know nothing about love, because they can't suffer, and in discussing love it is Adam, as the first human, whom we should honor.

pp. 112–13, Good news! The days of grief and pain

doorman: the chamberlain who grants or denies access to a king.

Jamshid: a legendary pre-Islamic Persian king, famous among other things for his longevity.

pp. 114–15, I'll say it openly, and be

both worlds: that is, this world and the world after death.

I am a bird from paradise: Hafez uses this metaphor in a number of poems; it was a stock motif in medieval Persian poetry.

This ruined monastery: a periphrasis for the world.

pp. 116–117, Ah, God forbid that I relinquish wine

Jamshid and Kavus: legendary pre-Islamic Persian kings.

pp. 118–19, Mild breeze of morning, gently tell

If Venus dances . . . Lord Jesus in the whirling dance: The planet/deity Venus is associated with music (her attribute is a harp or lute) and sensuality, Jesus with asceticism and spirituality; Venus is feminine, Jesus masculine; Venus as a deity belongs to the pre-Islamic, pagan world, Jesus represents a religion recognized by Islam as legitimate.

Their dance, which Hafez implies his poetry brings about, is a uniting of the physical and the spiritual, the feminine and the masculine, the pagan and the religiously legitimate; it also represents the cosmic "dance" of the turning of the heavens. Presenting the "lesser" of two figures (here the pagan, the feminine, the sensual) as the guide of the one who is apparently the "superior" is common in Sufi anecdotes. Together with the association of Jesus with Venus, which would be somewhat shocking to the religiously orthodox, this gives a Sufi feeling to the end of the poem.

pp.122–3, *My love's for pretty faces*

Don't scare me with your fire – that is, with your warning of how much love burns, or with your threat of hell-fire, or both.

but I / Lack mirrors to array / Myself – that's why I sigh: The last line (stanza in the translation) of this poem is obscure and has generated quite a lot of commentary. A mystical meaning would be that Hafez cannot prepare himself for the meeting with God (the common metaphor of the pure soul as a cleansed mirror seems to be involved, though exactly how is unclear). The line could also be read as saying "I lack recognition," in which case it can be seen as a bid for patronage. Two other perhaps relevant bits of information are that in a Persian wedding the bride sees her husband for the first time in a mirror, and that a sigh clouds a mirror (clouding a mirror is a negative metaphor in Sufi terms, involving sin, but it is also a sign of life). The line has obviously been thought obscure from early on, since an alternative last line for the poem turns up in some manuscripts.

pp. 126–7, The musky morning breeze

Nightingale will bring / His passion to the rose: See the note to p. 8.

Ramadan: See the note to pp. 16–17.

pp. 128–129, If that Shirazi Turk would take

Bokhara and Samarqand: two major cities of southern central Asia, which grew wealthy in the middle ages due to their position on the silk road linking East Asian and European trade. From 1369 Samarqand was the capital of Timur the Lame's (Tamburlaine's) empire. This line gave rise to the legend that in a meeting between Hafez and Timur (who had conquered much of Iran by the late 1380s; Isfahan fell in 1387), the conqueror reproached the poet by saying "These are two of my most splendid cities, and you would give them away for some pretty boy's mole?" Different versions of the anecdote record different witty responses by the poet to deflect Timur's anger: one is that he replied, "It is this ridiculous generosity of mine that has made me so poor"; another supposed response involves puns on the names of the cities; the poet says that what he was really proposing to give away was dates ("*khorma*") and sugar ("*qand*"). But by the time Timur was anywhere near Shiraz Hafez was in the very last years of his life, and though it is theoretically possible that they could have met it is extremely unlikely.

Mosalla and Roknabad: See the note to p. 32.

Alas, these rowdy, sweet-voiced gypsies: because orthodox Islam can be highly suspicious of music, musicians in medieval Iran were often non-Moslems (Gypsies were seen as, in origin at least, Indian pagans). Gypsies as musicians are recorded in the 11th century Persian epic the *Shahnameh*; Gorgani's romance, *Vis and Ramin*, from the same period, designates Jews as musicians. Music was thus linked with wine as something that was seen as the province of non-Muslims, and as Hafez shows a constant interest in both wine and music this reinforces the atmosphere of heterodox religious practices and beliefs that permeates much of his poetry.

Like Turks who make off with a feast's / Leftovers . . . : this line has generated considerable commentary. By Hafez's time, central Asian Turks had been slaves in southern Iran for centuries, but many of the ruling families of Iran also claimed a central Asian Turkish origin, and the word Turk could imply either subservience or royal authority. The reputation of Turkish conquerors as being ruthless and cruel was often transferred by poets to the erotic sphere, with the beautiful Turk – Turks had a reputation for beauty, largely because of their pale skin-color – being seen as treating his (or her) suitor in the same manner. It has been suggested that the Turks despoiling the feast is a metaphor for Timur's invasion of Iran, but other commentators have suggested a more mundane (and likely) explanation: "among some Turkomans it was the custom for the guests at a king's feast to be allowed to carry off the golden and sliver plate used there, once the feast was over" (commentary by Dr. Khalil Khatib-Rahbar, Tehran 1364/1985). The same commentator quotes a verse by Sa'di that uses a similar metaphor to Hafez's:

He has looted the heart of Sa'di and of the world
As men carry off the leavings of a king's New Year feast.

To tempt Zuleikha to discard: Zuleikha is the woman
known in the Bible as Potiphar's wife, who attempted
to seduce Joseph during his slavery in Egypt. As Joseph
became the archetype of male beauty in Persian poetry,
so Zuleikha became the archetype of one hopelessly
in love with such beauty. The trope often has mystical
overtones, with Joseph representing the beauty of God,
and Zuleikha representing the human soul trapped
in the world but longing for the divine. Sometimes
though, as primarily here, Zuleikha simply represents
reprehensible but all-too-understandable desire.

The pearl you've pierced is poetry's: See the note to p. 14.

pp. 130–31, Flirtatious games, and youth

Qavam: See the note to pp. 74–5.

JAHAN MALEK KHATUN

**pp. 138–9, O God, I beg you . . . / Each new flower . . . /
My heart will take . . .**

The three poems on these pages are taken from a
section of Jahan Khatun's *Divan* ("Collected Poems")
entitled "Elegy." The poems gathered together under this
title all apparently refer to the death of the same person,
named Sultan Bakht. It was once thought that the poems
lamented the death of Jahan Khatun's stepmother, who

was indeed named Sultan Bakht, and who seems to have been particularly close to the princess after the murder of her father. However, it's now accepted that the poems refer to the death of Jahan Khatun's daughter, who was also called Sultan Bakht (probably in honor of Jahan's stepmother), and who died at a very young age.

pp. 140–41, *I didn't know my value then, when I*

I took up lovers' chess, / And lost so many of love's pieces: Chess was a popular game at the medieval Persian courts, and Jahan Khatun mentions it a number of times – which suggests that it might have been one of her own pastimes – often, as here, as a metaphor for love.

pp. 142–3, *Here, in his beauty's garden, I –*

like the nightingale . . . sings the rose: See the note to p. 8.

pp. 144–5, *If you should kiss me with*

I'd be your slave and wear / Your earring in my ear: A slave's earring denoted to whom he or she belonged.

moon . . . cypress tree: The moon and the cypress are the commonest metaphors for a beautiful person (of either sex) in Persian poetry – the cypress for an elegant body, the (full) moon for the face.

pp. 146–7, *My heart is tangled like thick curls*

The stream that flows . . . Diminish over me: A garden and a tree, usually a cypress, beside a stream were important parts of what Jahan Khatun's contemporaries in Europe would have called a *locus amoenus* – that is, a pleasant place where pleasant things can be expected to happen, and life is, for the moment, enjoyable and good. A tree shading a stream in Persian poetry can be a metaphor for patronage and protection, and the juxtaposition can often, as here, take on erotic connotations, with the tree being the masculine element and the stream the feminine (a dream recounted in Gorgani's eleventh century romance *Vis and Ramin* has the same constituents, with the same implication of eroticism); the erotic dimension to the metaphor also involves the protective element of its "patronage" meaning. Obayd-e Zakani has a scurrilous version of the metaphor, which draws on and derides its romantic implications, in his poem "My prick's a cypress that grows tall and straight" on p. 211.

pp. 150–51, From now on I have sworn

His eyebrow's arch that's like / The new moon in its grace: See the note to p. 15.

like the nightingale . . . Harangues the rose: See the note to p. 8.

pp. 152–3, How sweet sleep is! I dreamed I saw

ka'abah: the black stone in Mecca, at the geographical center of the Islamic world, towards which Moslems pray and which is circumambulated by pilgrims.

I'm not a child to whom the world / Is still unknown: There is a pun on "Jahan" ("the world," and the poet's pen-name) in these last lines, which mean both "I know the world" and "I know myself."

p. 154, Come here a moment, sit with me, don't sleep tonight

this world's delight: As in the previous poem, there is a pun here on Jahan/world.

p. 155, How can I tell you what I want from you

How you hung on to love: "You" refers to the speaker's heart.

Men love the world . . . you shun: As in "How sweet sleep is! I dreamed I saw" (pp. 152–3), Jahan again puns on her name, meaning "world," so that these lines also mean "Men love Jahan, she's dear to everyone – So why's Jahan's love something that you shun?"

pp. 156–7, At dawn my heart said I should go

But your drunk eyes don't deign . . . love or drink: This stanza (line in Persian) depends on both a pun and an implied pun. The same Persian verb, which has a number of meanings, is translated as both "deign to" and "forgive." "Drunk" can mean simply drunk, but it can also mean "drunk with love," i.e. besotted with someone. "Drunk eyes," apart from the literal meaning, can also mean languorously attractive eyes, what we might call, "come-to-bed eyes." The line's implication is, "If it's easy for me to forgive you for being drunk, it should be easy for you to forgive me for being in love with you."

pp. 158–60, Suppose a breeze should bring to me

The Persian New Year falls at the spring equinox (March 20 or 21) and is traditionally a time of pleasure, picnics, and open-air festivities. The comparisons Jahan makes between flowers and different features of her beloved are all traditional, as is the notion that the flowers and trees will be abashed by his beauty and so be ashamed to show themselves. Violets are compared to dark, thick, glossy hair; narcissi are compared to eyes because their flowers have white outer petals with a dark brown center; the pinkish blossoms of the Judas tree (called in America the red-bud) are a metaphor for an attractive complexion, and so on. The picture of the spring blossoms drifting down on the lovers is also traditional, as is the notion of falling blossoms as tribute scattered before a prince, though the combination of the two images seems to be Jahan's own.

pungent musk / From Tartary: Musk, which was one of the most valued of medieval perfumes, is a glandular secretion of the musk deer; the most prized musk was imported from Tartary, the steppes of northern and central Asia.

p. 161, *O God be kind, and open wide your door*

This is clearly a poem written after Jahan's family's fall from power, as is made plain by the line "In one night, sovereignty abandoned me."

p. 162, *My friend, who was so kind and faithful once*

world's lord: "World" is a pun on the poet's name "Jahan," so that "world's lord" (i.e. God) also means "Jahan's lord" (i.e. the beloved addressed in the poem, who is implicitly compared to God, because for her, the phrase implies, he is like God).

p. 163, Have all your feelings for me gone?

world-destroying flower: a pun that also means "Jahan-destroying flower."

pp. 164–5, It will be God who opens up

Jahan Khatun's more religious poems, like this one, were probably written after her family's fall from power.

O world: This is a pun, as it also means "O Jahan," addressing herself.

pp. 166–7, How sweet those days when we were still

This poem would seem to have been written after Jahan's family's fall from power, when she was looking back on her lost youth, a time when she had been a pampered and relatively carefree princess.

famed / for our buildings' / bold magnificence: The north African traveler Ibn Battuta, who visited Shiraz during Abu Es'haq's reign, remarked on how the city's ruling families would compete with one another in the splendor of the buildings they erected (a situation very similar to that found in parts of medieval Europe, especially Italy).

We spread our light throughout the world: the poet's habitual pun on her name, Jahan/world.

pp. 168–9, How would it be, my soul's love, if you healed

You'll certainly upset the world: the poet's habitual pun on her name, Jahan/world.

p. 171, *Why is it you neglect me so? Why is it*

This poem is addressed to the conqueror of Shiraz and destroyer of the poet's family, Mobarez al-din (the "Mohammad Ghazi" of line 11). At its opening the poem looks as if it will be a conventional love poem, of a kind that is common in Jahan Khatun's *Divan*, complaining to a lover that he won't visit her, so that the shift to politics and anger, and the revelation of the real addressee as the poem progresses, is all the more effective because initially unexpected.

It's been suggested that this poem must have been written after the death of Mobarez al-din, (otherwise how could Jahan Khatun have dared to write it, given Mobarez al-din's known violence?). But the last lines suggest that Mobarez al-din is still alive and enjoying his power at the time of writing. It may be that the poet had left Shiraz, and was safely beyond her enemy's reach when the poem was written. The twice repeated pun on Jahan/world in the last stanza makes the poem not only mean "the world has deceived you and will see you are punished," but also, by implication, "I, Jahan, have deceived you and will see you are punished."

p. 172, *Most people in the world want power and money*

A poem that obviously refers to the political turmoil in Shiraz during the poet's lifetime; it was probably written after her family's fall from power. Towards its end the poem contains an example of the "swerve" (see note to pp. 74–5) sometimes found in medieval Persian poetry; the "Your," and the cypress, of the last four lines refer primarily to God rather than to an earthly deliverer, though the ambiguity is likely to be deliberate.

pp. 177–8, I am still drunk that you were here,

musk deer come / from Tartary: See the note to pp. 158–60.

p. 179, I know you think that there are other friends for me than you

You strike me like a harp, play on me like a flute: This line suggests that the addressee is sometimes brusque, or worse, with his beloved (the word translated as "strike" is the usual word for playing a stringed instrument, but it's also the usual word for hitting someone – how literally this is meant is not clear), and sometimes playful and cajoling; but whichever approach he takes, she accepts his behavior. Jahan is implying: "I put up with every kind of behavior from you, so what's the evidence that I'm tired of you, as you claim?"

p. 180, How long will heaven's heartless tyranny

This poem was probably written shortly after the conquest of Shiraz by Mobarez al-din. The "cypress" referred to in lines 7–8 is almost certainly Abu Es'haq, Jahan Khatun's uncle, and the king whom Mobarez al-din defeated and then had executed.

p. 181, Last night I dreamed I saw with Fortune's eyes

A poem in which Jahan Khatun remembers her family's lost power, and her own youth.

p. 182, Here, in the corner of a ruined school

The specificity of this, describing the poet waiting in a "ruined school" while her enemies, who are within earshot (presumably in the next room), decide what is to be done with her, is rare in Persian medieval poetry, and is all the more striking for that reason. Its most likely context is the events that happened in the aftermath of Mobarez al-din's victory. The extent of the school's ruins ("More ruined even than my heart") stands in for the destruction wrought on Shiraz by its rulers' constant squabbles and warfare (see the note to p. 16).

p. 188, My heart, if you have words you need to say

It is likely that this and the second poem on this page ("What has this life we long for given me? Tell me") were written after Jahan's family fell from power.

five times a day: referring to the five designated times each day for Moslem prayer.

p. 189, A picnic at the desert's edge, with witty friends

I'll grill his liver with my body's fiery heat: The image here can at first sight seem a little outré/off-key in English. The comparison of the feelings of someone in love to meat in the process of being grilled is a relatively common trope in Persian poetry. It's especially apt here for two reasons: 1) the liver is seen as the seat of the affections and of animal vitality (hence "I'll grill his liver" means, "I'll drive him crazy with desire"); and 2) the food at a picnic like the one described in the opening lines would certainly include grilled liver, which is still a tasty feature of outdoor meals in Iran. So Jahan

Khatun is playing with the two kinds of "liver"; this works without a problem in Persian, but whether it does so or not in English, I leave to the reader to decide.

p. 191, Pity the wretch, forced from her native land

This poem appears to have been written soon after Mobarez al-din killed her uncle, and Jahan's own life was in danger.

p. 192, Laughing, the rose said to the nightingale one day

The rose said to the nightingale: See the note to p. 8.

p. 193, My enemies' glib lies are never done

As in the Bible, the story in the Qur'an of Joseph's being sold into slavery by his brothers includes a detail of the brothers' telling their father that Joseph had been killed by a wolf.

OBAYD-E ZAKANI

pp. 196–7, I've set out from Shiraz, I've put

Obayd-e Zakani, who had a reputation for debauchery in a city where debauchery was fairly commonplace, not surprisingly left Shiraz during the reign of Mobarez al-din. This poem describes his reluctant journey from the city he had come to love more than his own hometown.

Like a nightingale . . . like a rose: See the note to p. 8.

pp. 199–200, The breeze of Mosalla, and Roknabad's

A poem in praise of Obayd-e Zakani's adoptive town, Shiraz. For Mosalla and Roknabad, and for Shirin and Farhad (here used as emblematic of a man hopelessly in love with an unapproachable princess), see the note to p. 32. The volte face at the poem's end, apparently rejecting the pleasures the poem has thus far celebrated, is an example of how Persian medieval poems are quite likely to end in a completely different place from where they seem to have been for most of their course (see also the note to pp. 74–5). This strategy is less common in western poetry but is not unknown (for example, the way that the final couplet in a Shakespeare sonnet can often turn away from or contradict everything that has been said before). In this poem, the turn appears as a compliment, and so it could be addressed to a patron or a lover, someone who by implication concentrates on purer things than mere sensual pleasure.

p. 203, Devil and then angel / I'm off to stroll through the bazaar . . .

Both the poems on this page demonstrate Obayd's equal-opportunity lasciviousness, one that is just as interested in girls as in boys. Because most more "serious" poets of the period, like Hafez and Jahan Khatun, are very rarely erotically specific, so that the gender of a partner in one of their poems is usually left unstated, in the original Persian, even by implication (see pp. xx–xxi), Obayd's poems are useful as examples of how the poetic conventions of the period can be used for talking about both sexes. It doesn't do to be dogmatic about the gender of a partner in a medieval Persian lyric poem. With a very few exceptions, it's usually impossible to say categorically that any given poem is about a boy or a girl; as Obayd insists, it might well be about either or both.

p. 207, Where is Shiraz's wine, that burned our grief away?

A poem presumably written after Mobarez al-din closed the wine-shops, and also clamped down on the use of "pretty boys."

p. 211, My prick's a cypress that grows tall and straight

Part of the effect of this poem is that it uses an elegant cliché of lyric poetry, the cypress growing by a stream (see the note to pp. 146–7), in a scabrous, mocking way.

p. 211, Ramadan's come – the time for passing wine around has gone

Ramadan: See the note to pp. 16–17.

pp. 214–15, The Lesson to be Learned from the End of King Sheikh Abu Es'haq

The poem begins as though it is in the middle of a typical example of a praise poem to a ruler, an extremely common medieval Persian poetic form. However, the tone changes from praise to lament halfway through, and we realize that it is an elegy, rather than simply a praise poem to a living ruler, written in hopes of a monetary reward. The subject of the poem is the overthrow by Mobarez al-din of King Abu Es'haq, the uncle of Jahan Khatun, and the patron of both Hafez and Obayd. Obayd assimilates the praise and lament to a third kind of Persian poem, that of versified advice. As is typical of works by Shirazi poets, the advice in question is to take the fall of kings as negative exempla, admonitions to stay far from courts, renounce ambition, and keep one's head down.

The names in the first half of the poem are of Persian kings notable for their splendor and power, to whom Abu Es'haq, while he was at the height of his glory, is being compared.

Qobad and Afrasyab: Legendary pre-Islamic kings who figure prominently in the eleventh-century epic *The Shahnameh*; Qobad ruled Iran while Afrasyab ruled Turan – that is, Central Asia. Obayd is implying that Abu Es'haq ruled both Iran and Central Asia; the fact that in reality he ruled little more than Fars, the province of which Shiraz was the capital, was no hindrance to this kind of hyperbole in court praise poetry.

An Ardavan, a Sanjar: Ardavan was almost the only Parthian king whose name had come down to medieval Iran (the Parthians ruled Iran from the mid-third century

BCE to the mid-third century CE); Sanjar (1085–1157) was the most successful ruler of the Seljuk Empire in Iran. Obayd perhaps brackets these two together because they both had the reputation of uniting the whole country.

Khosrow . . . Anushirvan: These were seen as the most ethically admirable of the kings whose exploits are chronicled in the legendary and historical sections of *The Shahnameh,* respectively. Anushirvan (the historical Sasanian king Nushin-Ravan, 501–79) was famous for his justice, and he was commonly called Anushirvan the Just. Another name for Anushirvan was Kasra, which is how Hafez refers to him in one of his poems (see the note to pp. 60–61) lamenting the fall of the Inju family. Interestingly, in these two poems, when they are condemning Mobarez al-din, Obayd and Hafez associate the same two pre-Islamic monarchs – Khosrow and Anushirvan/Kasra – with the defeated Inju kings.

that haunt of nightingales . . . whelping bitches: The court is implicitly compared to the "good place," the *locus amoenus,* of pleasure and safety, of which nightingales were usually a constituent part in medieval Persian poetry. A further implication is that Abu Es'haq was known as a patron of poets, including Obayd, and the "nightingales" of the court are his poets. The "black-hearted crow" is Mobarez al-din. Owls traditionally haunt ruins, and are seen as harbingers of death; the topos of animals giving birth in an abandoned palace is a common one in the poetry of the medieval period to indicate degradation and ruin. The dog is an unclean animal in Islamic societies, and the fact that it is dogs that are "whelping" in Abu Es'haq's palace indicates how low it has fallen.

The subject of *Cat and Mouse* is the same as that of the
previous poem, the conquest of Shiraz by Mobarez al-din.
The "cat" is obviously Mobarez al-din, and equally obviously
Abu Es'haq is the mouse king. The fact that the poem opens
with a mouse getting drunk might be an allusion to the
wine-loving culture of Shiraz under Abu Es'haq, something
that would have provoked the contempt of Mobarez al-din.
Obayd implies that the drunkenness of the mice leads
them to misjudge the threat the cat poses, and this perhaps
represents the Shirazis' self-indulgent carelessness in the face
of Mobarez al-din's enmity.

Obayd locates the cat's home in Kerman, in the southeast
of Iran, which was where Mobarez al-din was living when
feuding broke out between him and Abu Es'haq. (Mobarez
al-din was originally from near Yazd, in central Iran, but had
captured Kerman in 1340, and he used it from then on as his
center of operations, which mainly consisted of raiding and
terrorizing the surrounding cities.)

The cat's hypocritical professions of Islam, while killing
as many of the mice as he can, fit with reports of Mobarez
al-din's character, as being outwardly pious to the point of
asceticism, and also extremely brutal.

The mouse king draws his allies from Gilan, Rasht, and
Khorasan, northern areas that were friendly, or at least not
hostile to, the Inju family, from which Abu Es'haq came. The
more southern towns of Isfahan, Yazd, and Kerman, from
which the cat summons his cat allies, were all controlled by
Mobarez al-din himself or by members of his family. The
mouse ambassador probably represents Khajeh Emad-al
din, Abu Es'haq's emissary to Mobarez al-din before war

broke out between them. It is likely that many more references in the poem would have been be recognized by contemporary readers.

Cat and Mouse does not appear in the earliest manuscripts of Obayd's poetry, and this has led some scholars to doubt that it is actually by him, but it has always, from the medieval period on, been ascribed to him, and no other likely candidate has been suggested as its author. Its cynicism and bitter humor, its portrait of the cat's pious hypocrisy, its almost gleeful contempt for folly, together with the fairly intimate knowledge of Shirazi politics that it reveals, all fit well with what we know of Obayd, and with the atmosphere of many of his other poems, and so it seems reasonably safe to assume that the poem is Obayd's.

An interesting parallel, and perhaps remote precedent, to Obayd-e Zakani's *Cat and Mouse* is the Greek mock-heroic poem *The Battle of the Frogs and the Mice*, believed in antiquity to have been written by Homer himself, but now thought to be by an anonymous poet writing at around the time of Alexander the Great (the fourth century BCE). Obayd's poem seems quite close to *The Battle of the Frogs and the Mice* both in moments of its plot, and in the kind of rhetoric it employs. For example, the Greek poem begins with a mouse coming to drink, and being spied on by a frog who offers to help the mouse but then causes his death; another mouse escapes and runs home to tell the assembled mouse community of his friend's death at the hands of the frog (this becomes two separate incidents of the cat killing mice in Obayd's poem); the mice then decide to declare war on the frogs. The Greek poem diverges from Obayd's version in that its next incident involves the Olympian gods, who take sides in the ensuing war. But the two poems become similar again as they draw to a close: in both, the mice at first appear to win their war, but then a sudden reversal of fate (in the Greek poem engineered by the gods) takes away their victory. The poems are also about the same length (the Greek poem is a little longer, though omission of the passages about the gods, who don't figure in Obayd's poem, would bring it to around the length of *Cat and Mouse*), and they use similar kinds of mock-heroic rhetoric. It seems very unlikely that Obayd could have known of the Greek poem directly (it was written well over a thousand years before his time), but the twelfth-century Greek/Byzantine poet Theodoros Prodromos wrote a work in imitation of *The Battle of the Frogs and the Mice* called *The War of the Cat and the Mice*, and at first sight it seems plausible that it is this work that somehow found its way into the Persian cultural world and served, however remotely, as a model for Obayd's own tale of cat and mouse hostilities. But in fact the Byzantine work is quite far both in its plot and form (it's a play) from *The Battle of the Frogs and the Mice*, whereas the plot of Obayd's poem sticks (fairly) closely to that of *The Battle of the Frogs and the Mice*. Despite the Byzantine work's much greater proximity to Obayd's poem in time, and the similarity of the two works' titles, it seems probable that, if either of these works lies behind Obayd's poem, it is the more ancient poem that does so, and not the Byzantine play. How this might have come about is hard to say; it may be that this or similar tales circulated in Iran during the Hellenistic/Parthian period, and had survived, perhaps at an oral, folk level, until Obayd's time. Obayd's *Cat and Mouse* seems sui generis within Persian poetry, but a comparison with *The Battle of the Frogs and the Mice* suggests that he may have been adapting a traditional folk genre, perhaps ultimately deriving from Greek and/or Parthian models, to local political circumstances.

Appendix

Poems on Translating Hafez

My long preoccupation with Hafez's poetry has resulted in various attempts to formulate its nagging allure. Besides an essay in which I set out why I thought Hafez's verse was to all intents and purposes untranslatable ("On Not Translating Hafez," New England Review, Vol. 25, 1–2, 2004, pp. 310–18), I have also written three poems on the subject.

1

This poem was written when I first began to read Hafez seriously, some twenty years before writing the two poems that follow it. The figure in the poem is an amalgam of various British army officers and civil servants who tried their hands at translating Hafez while on duty in India; one such translator, who towers above all the others, was Lieutenant Colonel Wilberforce Clarke, of the Bengal Engineers, whose translation of the complete *Divan* of Hafez was published in 1891. His translation and commentary are a tour de force of both translation and scholarship, and have been very influential. Unfortunately for me, Wilberforce Clarke based his translation on a premise I think erroneous (that virtually all Hafez's poems have exclusively mystical meanings, so that anything quotidian in them – wine, roses, a nightingale, a lover, a wine-shop, ruins, and so forth – must be interpreted as symbolic of a mystical referent), which means that while I have great respect for his achievement, I don't feel it gets the Anglophone reader very close to what most of Hafez's poems are really like or about.

Translating Hafez

Northwest Frontier, 1880s

For V. L. Clarke

I SEE THE MAN I CONJURE — AT A DOORWAY
Bathed for a moment in the evening light
    And watching as the sun
    Descends behind bare hills

Whose shadow blurs, and renders substanceless,
Parade ground, barrack, flag-pole – the low step
    On which he stands; "the hour
    Of cow-dust," but no herds

Are brought in here to shelter from the dark:
The bright, baroque commotion of the sky
    Is simplified to dusk
    In which the first stars shine

Like an admonishment that stills the heart.
He enters the dark house: though he is here
    By accident he makes
    His being of that chance,

Set down within a country which he loves
And which, he knows, cannot love him – so that
  His homage is a need
  Become its own reward

Unprized as that which Aristotle says
Souls nurture for the irresponsive God:
  A barefoot servant brings
  The oil-lamp and his books

(And in another dispensation he
Would be that grave, respectful, silent child).
  Moths circle him and tap
  The lamp's bright chimney-glass;

Now seated at his desk he opens text
And commentary; he dips his pen and writes:
  "It is the night of power,
  The book of grief is closed ... "

2

This poem pretty well sums up my experience in trying to translate many of Hafez's poems over the past few years. It keeps fairly closely to the rules of the ghazal, as far as this is possible in English.

Translating Hafez, or Trying To

HOW LONG YOU'VE TEASED ME WITH YOUR TROPES, HAFEZ,
And led me on, and dashed my hopes, Hafez,

And left me like a foolish fog-bound man
Who pats and peers, and grasps and gropes, Hafez,

And thinks he's getting somewhere till he takes
A tumble down delusion's slopes, Hafez,

And nursing angry broken bones declares,
"God damn the guide, God damn the ropes, Hafez."

Your imperturbability is like
A really irritating pope's, Hafez –

But there, no matter how much Dick complains
Or goes off in a sulk, or mopes, Hafez,

Tomorrow finds him shaking (just once more)
Your glittering kaleidoscopes, Hafez.

The little incident described in the following poem happened exactly as recorded. *"Fal-e Hafez"* means "Divination by Hafez," which is still practiced in Iran, particularly but not exclusively during the celebrations of the Persian New Year at the spring equinox. The procedure is like that of the *Sortes Virgilianae* ("Divination by Virgil") as it was performed in Europe during the Middle Ages and Renaissance (a page of the poet's text is opened at random, and either the first line the eye lights on, or the line at the top of the page, is taken as advice, or as indicative of the future of the person who has opened the book). Both Virgil and Hafez were held in almost mystical esteem by the communities which used (in the Iranian case still use) their texts in this way, because they were thought to have access to hidden truths – Virgil because of his Fourth Eclogue, which was taken as a prophecy of the birth of Christ, Hafez because of the widespread mystical interpretation of his poetry, indicated by his common soubriquet "Tongue of the Unseen." I took my dog's jogging of my wrist, with its subsequent result, at the moment I was trying to decide on the literal or mystical meaning of "wine" in a particular line, as a parallel, if bathetic, kind of "Divination by Hafez."

At the time of writing, Daniel the spaniel is still alive and enjoying his daily walks, doggedly and blissfully unaware of his part in the interpretation of Hafez arcana.

A Daniel Come to Judgment
(*or* Fal-e Hafez)

HERE I WAS, STRUGGLING WITH A LINE
Of Hafez – was his longed-for wine
The real, red heady article
Or was it something mystical?
At this point my impatient spaniel
(Whose name is, for the rhyme's sake, Daniel),
Thinking a walk was overdue,
Nudged at my wrist, as dogs will do.
The glass I held splashed gouts of wine
Across the questionable line.
The wine was real; the blood-red blot
Said, "Mystical the wine is not."

Index of English First Lines

HAFEZ

Jahan Malek Khatun

Obayd-e Zakani

Index of Persian First Lines

About Dick Davis

As a translator, an eminent scholar of Persian literature, and an acclaimed poet in his own right, Dick Davis has published more than 20 books. Educated in England, he lived in Iran for eight years. He is a Fellow of the Royal Society of Literature and has taught at the University of California and Ohio State University. His recent translations include Ferdowsi's *Shahnameh: The Persian Book of Kings*, chosen as one of the "ten best books of 2006" by the *Washington Post*.

SOME OTHER MAGE TITLES

Vis and Ramin
Fakhraddin Gorgani / Translated by Dick Davis

Shahnameh: the Persian Book of Kings
Abolqasem Ferdowsi / Translated by Dick Davis

Borrowed Ware: Medieval Persian Epigrams
Introduced and Translated by Dick Davis

My Uncle Napoleon
Iraj Pezeshkzad / Translated by Dick Davis

At Home and Far from Home
Poems on Iran and Persian Culture
Dick Davis

They Broke Down the Door: Poems
Fatemeh Shams / Introduction and translations by Dick Davis

The Layered Heart: Essays on Persian Poetry
In Celebration of Dick Davis
Edited by Ali-Asghar Seyyed Ghorab

Stories from Iran: A Chicago Anthology 1921-1991
Edited by Heshmat Moayyad

Garden of the Brave in War
Terence O'Donnell

Crowning Anguish: Taj al-Saltana
Memoirs of a Persian Princess
Introduction by Abbas Amanat / Translated by Anna Vanzan

Discovering Cyrus: The Persian Conqueror
Astride the Ancient World
Reza Zarghamee